I'd like to thank my editors,
Jane O'Connor and Judy Donnelly,
who make the process of writing and revising
so much fun, and without whom
these books would not exist.

I also want to thank
Jennifer Dussling and Laura Driscoll
for their terrific ideas.

A Ghost Named Wanda

Text copyright © 1996 by Dan Greenburg.
Illustration copyright © 1996 by Jack E. Davis.
All rights reserved.

First published in the United States by Grosset & Dunlap, Inc., a member of Penguin Putnam Books for Young Readers under the title A GHOST NAMED WANDA.

No part of this publication may be reproduced, stored in a retrieval system, or transmitted, in any form or by any means, graphic, electronic, or mechanical, including photocopying, taping, and recording, without prior written permission from the publisher.
For information about permission, write to editor@ltinc.net

This Korean and English edition was published by Longtail Books, Inc. in 2020 by arrangement with Sheldon Fogelman Agency, Inc. through KCC(Korea Copyright Center Inc.), Seoul.

ISBN 979-11-93992-36-4 14740

Longtail Books

이 책은 ㈜한국저작권센터(KCC)를 통한 저작권자와의 독점계약으로 롱테일북스에서 출간되었습니다.
저작권법에 의해 한국 내에서 보호를 받는 저작물이므로 무단전재와 복제를 금합니다.

A Ghost Named Wanda

by Dan Greenburg
Illustrated by Jack E. Davis

For Judith, and for the real Zack,
with love—D.G.

Chapter 1

When the first **spooky** thing happened, I didn't even **realize** it was spooky. I don't know why, because I happen to like spooky things . . . unless they're really **scary** I mean, in which case maybe not so much.

Oh, I better tell you who I am. My name is Zack. I'm ten years old. And I guess I've always been sort of interested in **weird stuff**. Stuff like werewolves[1] and vampires[2] and zombies[3] and houses where you go into the bathroom and turn on the **faucet** and out comes **blood**. Stuff like that.

To be **honest** about it, I've never seen any of the things I just **mention**ed. But then I'm only ten years old.

Anyway, to get back to my story. One night a few months ago, I woke up suddenly. All the doors in our apartment kept on opening and closing. The door to Dad's room, my bedroom door, my

---

1 **werewolf** 늑대 인간. 전설이나 소설 등에 나오는 가상의 인물로 보름달이 뜨면 늑대로 변한다고 한다.
2 **vampire** 뱀파이어. 육체를 가지고 있으며, 무덤에서 일어나 살아 있는 인간의 피를 빨아서 그 생명력을 빼앗는다고 알려진 전설이나 소설 속의 가상의 존재.
3 **zombie** 좀비. 원주민의 미신과 공포 이야기에 나오는 되살아난 시체.

bathroom door, the door to my **closet**. Just opening and closing by themselves. I **figure**d, hey, **no big deal**. It's the wind or something. So I went back to sleep. If I had known what it really was, I probably wouldn't have been so **casual**.

When I woke up the next morning, the first thing I **notice**d was how **messy** my room was. Now I don't want you to get the wrong idea. My room is always pretty messy. But this morning, it was a lot messier than usual.

The pants I had taken off the night before and thrown on the floor were now hanging from the roller[4] of the window

---

4 **roller** 롤러. 창문 블라인드의 위에 달린 원통형의 대로 블라인드의 천 등을 감아 올린다.

shade. The shoes I had **toss**ed in the corner were in my **waste**basket. My T-shirt was hanging from the light on the **ceiling**. My **underpants** were on my teddy bear's[5] head. I was pretty sure I hadn't done any of these things. And I couldn't **imagine** who had.

I cleaned up the stuff as fast as I could. It wasn't so much because I like my room clean. I just didn't want my dad to come in and say, "What's wrong with this picture?" My dad is great, and I love him a whole lot. But he is kind of a **neat**ness **freak**. And I really can't **stand** when he comes into my room and says, "What's

---

5 **teddy bear** 테디 베어. 장난감 곰 인형으로, 미국의 26대 대통령 테어도어 루스벨트(Theodore Roosevelt)의 애칭을 따서 만들었다.

CHAPTER ONE

wrong with this picture?"

As soon as I cleaned up my room, I went to **brush** my teeth. And that's where I noticed some more **goofy** stuff. Somebody had **rub**bed soap all over my bathroom mirror. And put Saran Wrap[6] under the **toilet** seat. Had some kid **sneak**ed in to play **prank**s on me? Or was something weird going on here?

"Zack, you up?" my dad called from the **hallway**.

"Yeah, Dad," I called back.

He stuck his head in my bedroom door.

"Uh-oh," he said.

I went back into my bedroom, and my

---

6 Saran Wrap 사란 랩. 식품 포장에 사용되는 얇은 비닐 랩에 대한 상표명. 종종 일반적인 비닐 랩을 가리킬 때 사용하기도 한다.

mouth dropped open. My room was a **mess** again. Plus, all the **electrical cord**s were **tie**d into **bow**s. And a **frame**d photo of my Grandma Leah had a **moustache** and **beard** drawn on it. This was no kid playing pranks. Something weird was going on!

"What's wrong with this picture?" said my dad.

I could tell Dad was really **upset** by the mess. My mom and my dad **split** up a few years ago. Now I spend part of the time with him and part of the time with my mom. Dad's place has always been neater than Mom's. Up till now, that is.

"Dad," I said, "I just this minute cleaned my room, OK? Just before going into the bathroom to brush my teeth, I **swear**. I know this is going to sound crazy. But I think we're being **haunt**ed or something."

"Zack, I don't **mind** if you sometimes get **careless** and leave your room messy," said my dad. "But I really wish you wouldn't **fib** about it."

"I'm not fibbing," I said. "I really did clean up my room just a minute ago. I did not leave it like this."

The look on my dad's face told me he still wasn't **buy**ing it. But at that **precise** moment, the TV that sits on top of my **bookcase float**ed gently into the air. Then it flew slowly and silently across the room and **land**ed on my **dresser**.

My dad watched it go. His eyes were

very wide. So were mine.

"You know, Zack," said my dad after a long time, "I think I believe you **after all**."

Chapter 2

Dad and I ran out of my room and escaped into the kitchen. We **block**ed the door with a **stepladder**. Then we turned around.

Yikes! It was even worse in here!

The table was already set for breakfast. The only thing was, it was set **upside down**.

The **cupboard**s were open and empty.

All the dishes were **pil**ed up in one very tall **stack**, which was **sway**ing **unsteadily back and forth**.

There was no longer any **doubt** about it. We had a poltergeist.¹ I've read books about this **stuff**, and I know. But **in case** you don't, a poltergeist is like a ghost. A ghost that likes to cause trouble. They usually appear in homes with families that have at least one kid, and they **trash** the place.

I looked at my dad to see how he was taking all of this.

"What would you think of our staying

---

1 **poltergeist** 폴터가이스트. 독일어 'poltern(시끄러운 소리를 내다)'과 'geist(영혼)'이 합쳐져서 유래된 말로 '시끄러운 유령'이라는 뜻이다. 이상한 소리가 들리거나 물체가 스스로 움직이는 현상 등을 가리킨다.

in the Ramada **Inn**[2] tonight?" asked my dad.

"Oh, I don't want to spend the night in some strange **motel** room," I said.

Flapjacks[3] began cooking on the **stove**. They **flip**ped themselves up into the air. Then they turned over and **land**ed back in the **pan**.

The very tall stack of dishes **teeter**ed in one direction, then in the other. Then it **collapse**d with a very loud **crash**. Pieces of **smash**ed dishes flew in all directions.

The **refrigerator** door **sprang** open, and all the food inside **spill**ed out onto the

---

2 Ramada Inn 라마다 인. 세계적인 호텔 체인 가운데 하나.
3 flapjack 플랩잭. 밀가루에 달걀, 버터, 우유 등을 섞은 반죽을 프라이팬에 얇게 구워서 만드는 음식인 팬케이크를 부르는 다른 이름이다.

CHAPTER TWO

17

floor.

"**On the other hand,**" I said, "I hear those Ramada Inns can be really nice."

In school it was hard for me to do my work. And at the Horace Hyde-White School for Boys in New York City, there is a lot of work.

I kept thinking about ghosts. Who even knew what was going on now in my dad's apartment? I was thinking so hard about ghosts that I must have totally **tune**d **out** what we were doing in class.

At one point my English teacher, Mr. Hoffman, asked me something. I looked up, **startle**d.

"So, Zack," said Mr. Hoffman. "What's your **opinion**?"

"My opinion?" I said. I **clear**ed **my throat** and tried to **loosen** up my **tie**.

"Yes."

"Well," I said, **stall**ing for time, "you know, sir, there are so many ways to look at that question. I wouldn't want to **form** an opinion too quickly."

"Zack," he said, "it's *my* opinion that you have not been listening to our **discuss**ion."

"Uh, no, I guess I haven't, sir," I said. "I'm really sorry. But I have a lot on my mind today."

"Well, thank you for being so **honest**," he said. "What's on your mind today that's more important than schoolwork?"

"Poltergeists."

Some of the guys started laughing.

"Poltergeists?"

"Yes, sir," I said. "Do you happen to know anything about them?"

"Well," said Mr. Hoffman. "I know the word means 'noisy **spirit**' in German. But what made you think about poltergeists?"

"Well," I said, "I know this may sound hard to believe. But some **invisible force** is **wreck**ing my dad's apartment. And I thought it might be a ghost . . . a poltergeist."

CHAPTER THREE

The kids in class were laughing so hard they almost fell out of their chairs. "Oh, right, Zack," said some, and, "Yeah, sure, Zack."

"Anyone who believes in ghosts," said a kid named Vernon Manteuffel, "is a **superstitious** barfbag![1]"

There was more laughter.

"Shut up, Vernon," I said. Vernon Manteuffel **sweat**s a lot and only takes baths on weekends. He keeps his bubble gum behind his ear. He **brag**s that his **gym** clothes haven't been washed since the third **grade**. He's kind of a school **legend**.

"All right, boys, that's enough," said Mr.

---

1 **barfbag** 원래는 비행기 등에 비치된 구토 봉지라는 뜻이지만, 여기에서는 '멍청이'와 같은 욕설로 사용되었다.

Hoffman.

"You probably believe in the Tooth **Fairy**,² too," said Vernon Manteuffel.

"Shut up, Vernon," I said. I sure wish I could have thought of something cooler to say than shut up. But I couldn't.

"Why don't you *make* me shut up, barfbag," said Vernon.

"Zack! Vernon!" shouted Mr. Hoffman. "I do not **tolerate** fighting. One more word out of either of you and you are both staying after school."

Both Vernon and I got very quiet.

"That's better," said Mr. Hoffman. "You know, although I don't believe in

---

2 **Tooth Fairy** 이의 요정. 아이가 빠진 이를 머리맡에 두고 잠들면 밤에 나타나서 그것을 가져가고, 대신 동전을 놓고 간다는 상상 속의 존재.

the **supernatural**, there are a great many people who do. And they are not all superstitious barfbags either, Vernon. What I **suggest**, Zack, is that you go to the library and do a little **research**."

That was Mr. Hoffman's **solution** to every problem. Going to the library. **Come to think of it**, though, it wasn't a bad idea.

CHAPTER THREE

Chapter 4

After school I went straight to the **public** library. I looked up *ghosts* and *poltergeists* in the **encyclopedia**. It said some interesting **stuff**. But it didn't tell how to **get rid of** them. So I went to ask the **librarian** for help.

The librarian, Mr. Van Damm, has a thick **moustache** and very strong arms.

That is because he likes to **work out** a lot with **weight**s. He's a big, tough guy, but he really knows his **reference** books.

"Excuse me, sir," I said, "where **exact**ly would I find stuff about getting rid of ghosts?"

Mr. Van Damm **frown**ed at me. I hoped he didn't think I was **put**ting him **on**. He didn't seem like the kind of guy who liked being put on.

"You're serious?" he asked.

"I couldn't be more serious, sir," I said. "We have ghosts the way some people have **cockroach**es."

"Then what you want is a **banish**ing **ritual**," he said. "Banishing rituals are the **Roach Motels**[1] of the **spirit** world. You'll find them under *black magic*[2] over there under the **stairway**."

I thanked the librarian and went to look under the stairway for books on black magic. **In case** you don't know, pulling **bunnies** out of top hats[3] is called white magic.[4] Putting **curse**s on people or **fool**ing **around** with **evil** spirits is called black magic.

I read all about poltergeists. In one book on black magic, I finally found a

---

1 **Roach Motel** 로치 모텔. 미국에서 판매되는 바퀴벌레 퇴치 제품의 상품명이다. 먹이나 페로몬 등을 사용하여 바퀴벌레를 잡도록 고안되었다.
2 **black magic** 흑마술. 악령을 소환하거나 남을 저주하는 등의 비윤리적인 주술 행위를 말한다.
3 **top hat** 남자가 쓰는 정장용 서양 모자. 원통 모양에 실크 소재로 되어 있다. 마술쇼에서 주로 이런 모자를 사용해서 토끼가 사라지게 하는 마술을 선보인다.
4 **white magic** 선의의 마술. 흑마술과 반대되는 개념으로, 병을 치료하거나 다른 사람을 돕는 일에 사용되는 마술을 일컫는다.

banishing ritual. You **were supposed to** light seven black candles and say this seven times:

"O evil spirit, O great and terrible **demon** that **dwell**eth in **filth**, that liveth in dark, **stink**ing places, hear me now: I **cast** you **out**! I **command** you to **depart**! I **order** that you leaveth this place! O spirit who cometh in darkness, O demon of the **foul**est night, whose nose turneth backwards, whose face turneth **upside down**, whose clothes turneth **inside out** so that his underwear doth[5] show, **rouse** yourself and be gone from this place

---

5 dwelleth, liveth, leaveth, cometh, turneth, doth 동사 뒤에 '-(e)th'가 붙는 것은 고어에서 동사의 3인칭 단수 현재형의 어미 변화를 나타내던 것으로 현대 영어의 '-(e)s'에 해당된다.

immediately!"

It sounded to me like these evil spirits were all dead guys from **ancient** England or something. And maybe that was the only language they'd understand. I didn't think you'd need to talk to American dead guys like that. **On the other hand,** maybe the spirit that was **trash**ing my dad's apartment *was* an old dead guy from ancient England. In that case, it would understand us.

I took my book to the **checkout** desk. I was in line behind a big kid who also had a **load** of books on ghosts and evil spirits. The kid was **sweat**ing like crazy.

"Vernon!" I said. "What are you doing with those books? You said anyone who believes in ghosts is a **superstitious barfbag**."

Vernon's eyes **bugged out** when he saw it was me. He was so red in the face, I thought he might **pop** a **vein**. "I *d-don't* believe in that stuff," he **stammer**ed.

He sure didn't sound too **convincing**.

"Then why are you **check**ing **out** books on ghosts?"

"If I tell you, do you promise to keep it a secret?"

"Maybe."

"Here's the thing," Vernon said, looking around **nervous**ly and lowering his voice to a **whisper**. "Something **weird** is going on in *my* apartment, too."

"You mean **invisible force**s have been

trashing your place?" I asked, **amaze**d.

"No, worse than that, Zack," he said. "Much worse. Invisible forces have been **straighten**ing it up."

"That doesn't sound so bad to me," I said, remembering what was going on in my dad's apartment.

"You don't understand," he said. "Things in my room are being invisibly **rearrange**d. Not the way I want them, but the way something else wants them. I get out of bed; it **make**s **itself**. The **sheet**s and **blanket**s **tuck** themselves in so tight you could **bounce** a quarter[6] on top of them. Sometimes that happens while I'm still

---

6 quarter 쿼터. 미국·캐나다의 25센트 동전.

CHAPTER FOUR

33

in bed. Zack, do you think we've got a poltergeist?"

"If you do," I said, taking my book and heading toward the door, "it's even weirder than the one we've got."

"Hey, Zack!" he said. "Can't you help me?"

"I'll **check in with** you later," I said.

I left Vernon on the steps of the library. If the banishing ritual worked for me, maybe I'd show Vernon how to do it too. Not that he's my favorite person, as I said before. But I did sort of feel sorry for him—having to live with all that **neat**ness, I mean.

I stopped off at the party store[7] on the corner. I bought seven black candles. Then

I headed over to my dad's apartment to do the banishing ritual. I **was**n't all that **hot to** talk to dead guys, especially evil ones. But I felt it was our only hope.

---

7 **party store** 풍선이나 장식용품 등 파티에 필요한 물품을 판매하는 가게.

CHAPTER FOUR

Chapter 5

When I returned home with my book on black magic and my seven black candles, my dad was **freak**ing out.

At first I thought he was mad at me for being late. But then I saw that wasn't it at all. Things in the apartment had gotten a lot worse. Not only was the place **complete**ly trashed, but there was clear gooey stuff all over everything. It looked like a **combination** of maple syrup[1] and **rubber** cement.[2]

"What *is* this stuff?" my dad **croak**ed. He was so **upset** he could **barely** speak.

"I just read about this at the library," I said. "This is what they call *ectoplasm*.[3] It's something that appears when there are spirits around."

I felt **horrible** for my dad and what had happened to his nice apartment. His eyes got kind of **glassy**. He looked like a guy in a war movie. **Shell-shocked. Wobbly** on

---

1 **maple syrup** 메이플 시럽. 단풍나무의 수액을 졸여서 만든 밝은 갈색이 나는 시럽.
2 **rubber cement** 고무 접착제. 탄성이 있는 고분자에 아세톤, 헥산 등의 용매를 섞어 만든 접착제로 가죽이나 금속 등을 붙이는 데 사용된다.
3 **ectoplasm** 엑토플라즘. 심령 현상에서 사용되는 용어로 혼령과 소통하면 생긴다는 끈적거리는 가상의 물질을 말한다.

his legs.

I knew I had to take **charge**. I showed him the book on black magic and told him we were going to do a **banish**ing **ritual**. He **nod**ded, **staring** straight ahead.

Then we lit the seven black candles. And I began to read aloud in a voice I hoped sounded more **confident** than I felt: "O **evil** spirit, O great and terrible **demon** that **dwell**eth in **filth**, that liveth in dark, **stink**ing places, hear me now. . . ."

I **went on** and on. But nothing happened. Nothing. So I stopped reading, **slam**med down the book, and looked at Dad.

"I'm sorry," I said. "This isn't working."

That's when we heard a very loud noise. A big bag of peanut M&Ms[4] that was on a **shelf** just kind of **explode**d. All the M&Ms flew upward. They hit the **ceiling**, and stuck there. The way they stuck **spell**ed out a message. It said:

OK OK, HERE I AM WHAT NOW?

"Oh, my gosh," I said softly.

"Oh, my gosh," said my dad.

I couldn't believe it. I had made **contact** with an actual evil spirit, with an actual spirit of a dead person.

If you want to know the truth, I got very **scare**d. I felt a terrible **chill**, like I had just opened the **freezer** to get some **frozen** yogurt,[5] and all of the coldness

---

4 **M&M** 세계적으로 판매되는 작고 둥근 모양의 초콜릿 캔디. 초콜릿이 다양한 색의 설탕 코팅 속에 들어 있으며, 옆면에 알파벳 m이 새겨져 있다.

5 **frozen yogurt** 프로즌 요구르트. 요구르트나 유제품 등을 재료로 한, 얼려서 먹는 후식으로 아이스크림과 유사하다.

CHAPTER FIVE

just fell out on top of me. The skin on my head and on my back and neck began to **tingle**.

"What do we do now?" I **whisper**ed.

"I don't know," said my dad. His voice was still kind of **shaky**. But he looked less **daze**d. "Why don't you ask it something?" he said.

"O spirit who dwelleth in this place," I said in a low, **respectful tone**. "Are you the same spirit who hath trashed our apartment?"

There were soft, **scraping** sounds as the M&Ms on the ceiling re**arrange**d themselves into a new pattern. It said:

A RILLY DUM QUESCHUN

"I can't believe it," I whispered to

my dad. "We're actually having a **conversation** with a dead guy!"

"Not only with a dead guy," said my dad. "With a dead guy who can't spell." At least Dad was sounding like his old self again.

"O spirit," I said, "why dost[6] thou[7] doeth these things to us?"

There were more soft, **scratch**ing sounds above our heads, and then a new arrangement of M&Ms:

FRANKLY IM BORD ALSO ITS FUN

"But you're **ruin**ing all our **furniture** and dishes and stuff," I said. "If thou

---

6 **dost** 동사 'do'의 고어로 2인칭 주격 대명사 'you'의 고어 'thou'와 함께 사용된다.
7 **thou** 2인칭 주격 대명사 'you(너는)'의 고어.

keepeth this **up**, we'll have nothing left."

TUFF ITS MY JOB

"It's your job?" I said. "What's your job?"

More soft, scratching sounds.

2 B[8] MISHEVUSS MISCHIVISS MISCHEFUSS[9] O THE HECK[10] WITH IT 2 MAKE A **MESS** OF THINGS

This evil spirit was about the worst speller I had ever met, alive or dead.

"Dad, I don't know what else to ask it," I whispered.

"We should find out whom we're talking

---

8 **2 B** 본문에서 완다는 'to be'를 발음이 비슷한 숫자 2와 알파벳 B를 사용하여 표현했다.
9 **mishevuss mischiviss mischefuss** 형용사 'mischievous(짓궂은)'의 철자를 완다가 잘못 말한 것이다.
10 **heck** '도대체', '젠장' 또는 '제기랄'이라는 뜻으로 당혹스럽거나 짜증스러운 감정을 강조하는 속어.

to," said my dad.

"O spirit, what art[11] thy[12] name?" I asked. "I mean, to what name dost thou answereth?"

There was another quick arrangement of M&Ms:

WANDA

"Wanda?" I repeated. "But Wanda is a woman's name."

SO WHAT

"You're a woman?" I said.

SO WHAT

"Uh, about how many hundred years old art thou, ma'am?" I asked.

ABOUT 8

---

11 art 동사 'are'의 고어로 2인칭 대명사의 고어와 함께 사용된다.
12 thy 2인칭 소유격 대명사 'your(너의)'의 고어.

"Thou art eight hundred years old?" I asked respectfully.

NO JUST 8 SILY 8 AND A HAFF GOING ON 9

"Eight and a half?" I said. "Dad, it's a kid! A kid has been trashing our apartment!"

"Well, I guess that **makes sense**," said my dad. "I mean, it makes about as much sense as talking to dead people who speak through peanut M&Ms and who can't spell."

"If you're dead," I said, "why aren't you in heaven or someplace like that?"

LONG WATING LIST TO GET IN

"How come you chose this apartment to trash?" I asked.

I USE TO LIVE HEAR

"You lived in this building?" said my dad.

YEH ABOUT THIRDY YEARS AGO I HATED IT

"Why did you hate it?" I asked.

NOBODY TO PLAY WITH THEN ETHER NOBODY WAS MY FREND

I was trying to think of what to say to Wanda next, when suddenly my Game Boy[13] went **sail**ing through the air. It **smash**ed into the wall and broke into around a thousand pieces. I loved my Game Boy. I had almost gotten to the 29th level of "**Teen Master**s of the **Galaxy**" on

---

13 **Game Boy** 게임 보이. 닌텐도(Nintendo)에서 출시한 소형 휴대용 게임기로 선풍적인 인기를 끌었다.

it. Now it was completely **wreck**ed.

"Wanda, you **jerk**, why did you do that?" I shouted.

The M&Ms on the ceiling rearranged themselves again:

JUST FELT LIKE IT GOT BOARD

"You know what I think?" I said. "I think you're a **troublemaker** and a jerk. I think you were a troublemaker and a jerk even *before* you were dead. That's why you didn't have friends. You keep acting like a jerk and you're not ever going to have friends for the whole rest of your **afterlife!**"

Chapter 6

"Wanda seems to be an unhappy kid," said my dad. "Maybe I should try talking to her."

"Go ahead," I said. I sat down and **cross**ed my arms. I wanted nothing more to do with Wanda.

"Wanda," said my dad, in this really **calm** voice, "I think you must be very angry to be **trash**ing our apartment."

HA HA HA WHO EVEN CARES WHAT YOU THINK

"What do you think could be making you so angry?" my dad **went on**.

IM DED

"Well then, why don't you go and play with some nice *dead* girls and leave us alone!" I couldn't help **yell**ing.

THERE AINT NONE AROUND

"Tough![1]" I said.

"Zack, you're not being **helpful**," Dad **point**ed **out** in a sharp voice. Then he turned his face back to the **ceiling**. "Wanda, what can we do?" he asked.

---

1 **tough** '힘든', '강인한'이라는 일반적인 의미가 아니라, 여기에서는 '설마!'라는 뜻으로 사용되었다.

There was no reply for several moments. Then the M&Ms rearranged themselves once more:

I WANT ZACK TO PLAY WITH ME

I was **amaze**d. I couldn't believe it.

"Why the heck would I ever want to play with somebody who **destroy**s my toys and **wreck**s my dad's apartment?" I said. "You think I'm **nuts**? I only play with people who **treat** me nicely and who treat my **stuff** nicely. And that sure isn't you!"

Once again Wanda was slow in answering. Then the M&Ms **shift**ed into a new **combination** of letters:

WHAT IF I COUD FIX IT

I looked at my dad. He looked around our wrecked apartment and shook his head sadly.

"Wanda," I said, "this place looks like a **war zone**. What you've done to our apartment is beyond fixing."

WANNA **BET**

"Yeah," I said.

HOW MUCH

"A quarter," I said. I took out a quarter and held it up. "Here's my money."

The quarter I was holding turned **tingly** and **disintegrate**d. Then there was a **blind**ing **flash**. All the pieces of my Game Boy flew back together again. It was just like in a TV **commercial** when they **run** the film in **reverse** and somebody jumps backward out of a swimming **pool**, onto the **diving** board.

"Holy cow,[2]" I said. "How did you do that?"

TRIX OF THE **TRADE**

"Listen, Wanda, could you fix the rest of the stuff you broke?" Dad asked in a **hopeful** voice.

THAT **DEPENDS**

"On what?"

ON WHAT ZACK DOES FOR ME

I looked at my dad. He **shrug**ged. Then I had an idea. I didn't think I wanted to **hang out with** Wanda. She wasn't **exact**ly my type, being dead **and all**, but . . .

"Hey, Wanda," I said, "if you fix the rest of the stuff you broke, I might just be

---

2 holy cow '세상에', '이런', '맙소사' 등 놀람이나 곤혹스러움을 나타내는 표현.

able to find you a possible **playmate**."

YOU MEAN YOU

"No no, not me. Better than me. Somebody in the **spirit** world. What do you say?"

There was no reply. I wondered if Wanda had heard me. Then the room began to **shudder,** as if a **major earthquake was about to** begin. The whole apartment grew kind of **hazy,** like in a **sandstorm.** And then suddenly things started flying through the air. Dishes. **Silverware. Plate**s. **Pan**s. Clothes. Books. TV sets. There were **horrid** sounds. **Scraping. Grind**ing. **Clang**ing.

A heavy book **bounce**d off my left shoulder. A **glob** of ectoplasm **land**ed on my **cheek**. A small dish flew past my ear like a flying **saucer**.³ **Come to think of it**, it *was* a flying saucer.

And then, as suddenly as it had begun, it was over. The haze **lifte**d. My dad and I looked around the apartment. We couldn't **believe our eyes**.

The **gooey** ectoplasm was **complete**ly gone. The kitchen was all cleaned up, too. In my room, things weren't what you would call **neat**. But it was **certain**ly no **messier** than before Wanda had gone to work.

I was so happy I wanted to yell. My dad looked like he'd just won the **lottery** or

---

3 **flying saucer** 비행접시. 정체를 알 수 없는 비행 물체를 가리키는 말로, 주로 접시 모양으로 알려진 데서 붙은 이름이다.

something.

"Wanda, you did it!" I said. "You really did it!"

I TOLD YOU

"Well," I said, "you did what you said. So now I'll do what I said. Follow me."

WHERE WE GOIN

"You'll see," I said.

CHAPTER SIX

Chapter 7

My dad was so **thrill**ed the apartment was back together again, he was happy to let me go to Vernon's. And when I called Vernon and told him I was coming to help him with his poltergeist, he couldn't believe it.

So I took my book of black magic and my seven black candles. And I walked the three **block**s to Vernon's, looking both ways when I **cross**ed the streets. I kept talking to Wanda. I wanted to make sure she was following me. I couldn't see her, of course. And because there were no M&Ms around, she couldn't "talk" to me. People I passed on the street saw me speaking to somebody who wasn't there. They looked at me like I was **cuckoo**.

"Yo, Wanda," I said, "if you're still with me, give me a **sign**."

A very **stuffy**-looking lady, wearing a **straw** hat with a wide **brim**, was walking toward me. **All of a sudden** something **grab**bed the brim of her straw hat and **yank**ed it down over her eyes. Yep! Wanda was still with me!

A man smoking a fat, **stink**ing cigar[1] saw this and began to laugh. And then his cigar **explode**d in a **shower** of **spark**s, **cover**ing his face with black **soot**.

Soon I was at Vernon's apartment. Vernon's **folk**s were rich. Their huge Fifth Avenue[2] apartment was filled with huge sofas, huge glass tables, and huge uncomfortable chairs. Most of their **furniture** was covered with clear plastic covers. Probably Vernon's folks **sweat**ed as much as he did.

Right away I saw the problem. His apartment was a lot **neat**er than

---

1 **cigar** 시가. 담뱃잎을 썰지 않고 통째로 돌돌 말아서 만든 담배.
2 **Fifth Avenue** 미국 뉴욕시의 5번가(街). 뉴욕 맨해튼(Manhattan)을 남북으로 종단하는 가장 번화한 거리로 고급 아파트나 고급 상점들이 들어서 있다.

apartments ought to be. All the magazines on the coffee table kept re**arranging** themselves, first by size and then by date. And a **dust rag** with nobody holding it was **polish**ing all the **fancy stuff** in the front **hall**.

"Hey, Vernon," I called, "where are you?"

The minute I said that, the dust rag stopped polishing and **float**ed off down the **hallway**. It was going toward the back of the apartment. I **realize**d I **was supposed to** follow.

Vernon was eating dinner in the kitchen, **slurp**ing up alphabet soup. As I watched, the letters in the soup kept rearranging themselves so that they went into his spoon in perfect **alphabetical order**.

"Zack, would you like some dinner?" asked his mom.

"No thanks, Mrs. Manteuffel. I think we should get straight to work."

We lit the seven black candles. Then I opened the book of black magic and began to read the **banish**ing **ritual** again: "O **evil spirit**, O great and terrible **demon** that **dwell**eth in **filth**, that liveth in dark, stinking places . . ."

All at once there was a small explosion. A piece of paper dropped onto the kitchen table, and a pen flew out of a desk **drawer** and began writing in a very fancy **handwriting**.

"**Kindly** do not **insult** me," it wrote. "I am not evil. I do not dwell in filth. And I

most **certain**ly do not live in dark, stinking places!"

Vernon and his mom **stare**d at the pen **scribbling** away on the piece of paper. Their eyes almost **pop**ped right out of their heads.

"Vernon," said his mom. "I didn't know you knew magic **trick**s. How did you do that?"

"It wasn't me!" said Vernon.

"Forgive me, spirit," I said. "I can see that you are very clean and neat. What is your name?"

"You may **address** me as Cecil," wrote the pen. "And by what name shall I address you, sir?"

"I'm Zack," I said. Nobody had ever

called me "sir" before. I sort of liked it.

"I am **pleased** to make your **acquaintance**, Zack," wrote the pen. "But whom have you brought with you? I **sense** the **presence** of another spirit."

There was another small explosion. A box of Cheerios[3] fell out of a kitchen **cupboard**. Its **content**s flew onto the table where Vernon was eating his dinner. As Vernon, his mother, and I watched, the Cheerios arranged themselves into words:

HEY CECIL IM WANDA HOWYA DOIN

---

3   **Cheerios** 치리오스. 미국의 유명 시리얼 브랜드로 통귀리로 만든 시리얼이 특징이다.

Chapter 8

The pen began **scribbling** messages to Wanda. And the Cheerios kept re**arranging** themselves into messages to Cecil. The scribbling and rearranging went faster and faster. Pretty soon it was too fast for any living person to follow.

"Well," I said, "I guess those two have **hit it off.**"

The scribbling and rearranging of Cheerios **skid**ded to a stop. Then the Cheerios **spell**ed out something slowly enough for me to read it:

THATS WHAT YOU THINK

"You mean you don't like each other?" I said.

The pen began to scribble again.

"Your friend Wanda is a **crude, uneducated**, and **unacceptably messy** person," it wrote.

The Cheerios came alive.

YOUR FREND CECIL IS A **SNOB**

"Hey, come on, guys," I said. "You two have so much in **common**, being dead **and all**."

"Yeah, you two *have* to **get along**!"

Vernon added.

VERNIN YOU ARE A JURK WHO SWEATS A LOT, said the Cheerios.

"Hey!" said Vernon, getting up from his chair. "**Take** that **back!**"

Suddenly Vernon's pants were **yank**ed down to his shoes. He had on **underpants** with purple **dinosaur**s. He quickly **bent** over to pull his pants back up. But before he could **reach** them, they were pulled **violent**ly up his legs and into place again. And his shirt was **tuck**ed in tight by **unseen** hands.

"**Cut** that **out!**" said Vernon.

"Stop that!" said Vernon's mother.

Vernon's pants were once more yanked down to his shoes. And then up again.

And then down again just as fast.

"Wanda! Cecil! Stop it this **instant!**" I shouted.

It was louder than my dad **yell**s when he's really angry. It was louder than Mr. Hoffman yelled when Vernon and I had our fight in class. It was so loud that Vernon and his mother were shocked into silence.

I guess Wanda and Cecil were too, because Vernon's pants stopped moving up and down his legs like a yo-yo.[1] He pulled them back up again and sat down.

"That's better," I said. "You two may be dead, but you're acting like babies. And I

---

1 yo-yo 요요. 둥글고 납작한 두 개의 작은 원반을 연결한 짧은 축에 실을 감아 그 끝을 손에 쥐고 던졌다 당겼다 하면서 가지고 노는 장난감.

will not **tolerate** it."

Mr. Hoffman likes to use the word "tolerate" a lot. I can see why.

"OK," I said. "Look, you two could be great friends. But you have to learn to get along. If you try to, you can. I mean Vernon and I are getting along now. And we don't even like each other."

"Hey!" said Vernon. He looked **hurt**.

"I mean we didn't *before*," I said. "Anyway, you have to get along. You don't have any choice. There just aren't that many dead kids in the **neighbor**hood. Also, you need to find a place to stay."

HOW BOUT WE MOVE IN WITH YOU ZACK

"Yeah, Zack," said Vernon, "that's a

great idea."

"Sorry, guys," I said. "**No way.**"

"What about the two of us **residing** with Vernon?" scribbled the pen.

"Now *there's* an interesting idea," I said.

"No way!" yelled Vernon, jumping up from the table. For a moment there, I thought he was going to lose his pants again.

"OK, **gang**, I've got an idea," I said. "You know the Adventureland **Amusement Park** right across the river in New Jersey?[2] Well, they've got a **haunt**ed house in it that is really **pathetic**. It couldn't even **scare** a five-year-old. But a

---

2 **New Jersey** 뉴저지주(州). 미국 동북부에 위치한 주로 섬유, 금속, 조선 등의 공업이 발달하였다.

couple of **pros** like you could really **whip it into shape in no time**. Why,[3] after you two start haunting it, I'll **bet** that place could **scare the daylights out of** anybody."

OR THE PANTS[4]

"Yeah," I said. "So what do you say, guys? Are you **willing** to move to Adventureland?"

There was no reply at first. And then: "I believe that **taking over** the haunted house at Adventureland would be an **intriguing challenge**," wrote the pen.

Vernon and his mom looked **relieved**.

"What about you, Wanda?" I said.

---

3 **why** 여기에서는 이유를 묻거나 말할 때 쓰는 의문사 또는 관계사가 아닌 '어머, 아니'라는 뜻의 감탄사로 쓰였다.

4 **the pants** 숙어 'scare the pants off(남을 놀라게 하다)'에서 나온 표현으로, 잭이 말한 'scare the daylights out of'와 같은 뜻이다.

WOOD YOU COME TO VISIT US

"Uh, well, sure," I said. "You bet we would, Wanda. We'll visit you whenever we get a chance."

IF YOU DONT VISIT US THEN I GUES WELL HAVE TO VISIT YOU

"We'll visit you, we'll visit you," I said.

And so Wanda and Cecil went off to live in the haunted house at Adventureland. I wonder if they found a way to get along! Every once in a while on the news, I hear about strange things going on out there. Everybody thinks the people who **run** Adventureland just **dream**ed **up** some new **spooky trick**s. But I know who's really behind it.

And I'm keeping my promise to Wanda.

We're **celebrating** my next birthday with a big party in the haunted house at Adventureland.

It should be an interesting party. Very interesting, in fact.

CHAPTER EIGHT

THE ZACK FILES™ Series

1. Great-Grandpa's in the Litter Box
2. Through the Medicine Cabinet
3. A Ghost Named Wanda
4. ZAP! I'm a Mind Reader
5. Dr. Jekyll, Orthodontist
6. I'm Out of My Body . . . Please Leave a Message

THE ZACK FILES™

A Ghost Named Wanda

My room is a mess.

Now usually this is not big news.

But my clothes have started moving . . .

when I'm not inside them.

And the TV is floating across the room!

Guess what! I'm sharing my room

with a ghost named Wanda.

by Dan Greenburg
Illustrated by Jack E. Davis

CONTENTS

The Zack Files • 4

Chapter 1
• Quiz & Words List ·· 10

Chapter 2
• Quiz & Words List ·· 18

Chapter 3
• Quiz & Words List ·· 24

Chapter 4
• Quiz & Words List ·· 30

Chapter 5
• Quiz & Words List ·· 40

Chapter 6
• Quiz & Words List ·· 50

Chapter 7
• Quiz & Words List ·· 60

Chapter 8
• Quiz & Words List ·· 68

번역 • 76
Answer Key • 94

THE ZACK FILES

평범한 소년이 겪는 기상천외하고 흥미로운 모험을 그린 이야기, 잭 파일스!

『잭 파일스(The Zack Files)』 시리즈는 뉴욕에 사는 평범한 소년 잭이 겪는 때로는 으스스하고, 때로는 우스꽝스러운 모험을 담고 있습니다. 저자 댄 그린버그(Dan Greenburg)는 자신의 아들 잭에게서 영감을 받아 그를 주인공으로 한 이야기를 떠올렸고, 잭과 같은 아이들이 독서에 흥미를 갖기를 바라는 마음을 담아 이 책을 썼습니다.

초자연적인 현상에 대한 저자의 관심을 녹여 낸 『잭 파일스』 시리즈는 누구나 한 번쯤은 들어 본 기괴한 이야기들을 아이들이 재미있게 읽을 수 있도록 흥미진진하게 소개하고 있습니다. 현재까지 총 30권의 책이 출간되어 전 세계 아이들의 호기심을 불러일으키고 있으며, 동명의 TV 드라마로도 제작되어 많은 관심과 사랑을 받기도 했습니다.

이러한 이유로 『잭 파일스』 시리즈는 '엄마표·아빠표 영어'를 진행하는 부모님과 초보 영어 학습자라면 반드시 읽어야 하는 영어원서로 자리 잡았습니다. 간결한 어휘로 재치 있게 풀어 쓴 이야기는 영어원서가 친숙하지 않은 학습자들에게도 즐거운 원서 읽기 경험을 선사할 것입니다.

번역과 단어장이 포함된 워크북, 그리고 오디오북까지 담긴 풀 패키지!

이 책은 영어원서 『잭 파일스』 시리즈에, 탁월한 학습 효과를 거둘 수 있도록 다양한 콘텐츠를 덧붙인 책입니다.

- **영어원서**: 본문에 나온 어려운 어휘에 볼드 처리가 되어 있어 단어를 더욱 분명하게 인지할 수 있고, 문맥에 따른 자연스러운 암기 효과를 얻을 수 있습니다.
- **단어장**: 원서에 볼드 처리된 어휘의 의미가 완벽하게 정리되어 있어 사전 없이 원서를 수월하게 읽을 수 있으며, 반복해서 등장하는 단어에 '복습' 표기를 하여 자연스럽게 복습을 돕도록 구성했습니다.
- **번역**: 영문과 비교할 수 있도록 직역에 가까운 번역을 담았습니다. 원서 읽기에 익숙하지 않은 초보 학습자도 어려움 없이 내용을 파악할 수 있습니다.
- **퀴즈**: 챕터별로 내용을 확인하는 이해력 점검 퀴즈가 들어 있습니다.
- **오디오북**: 본문 전체에 대한 오디오북을 포함하고 있어, 듣기 훈련은 물론

소리 내어 읽기에까지 폭넓게 사용할 수 있습니다.

『잭 파일스』, 이렇게 읽어 보세요!

- **단어 암기는 이렇게!** 처음 리딩을 시작하기 전, 오늘 읽을 챕터에 나오는 단어들을 눈으로 쭉 훑어봅니다. 모르는 단어는 좀 더 주의 깊게 보되, 손으로 쓰면서 완벽하게 암기할 필요는 없습니다. 본문을 읽으면서 이 단어를 다시 만나게 되는데, 그 과정에서 단어의 쓰임새와 어감을 자연스럽게 익히게 됩니다. 이렇게 책을 읽은 후에 단어를 다시 한번 복습하세요. 복습할 때는 중요하다고 생각하는 단어들을 손으로 쓰면서 꼼꼼하게 외우는 것도 좋습니다. 이런 방식으로 책을 읽으면 많은 단어를 빠르고 부담 없이 익힐 수 있습니다.

- **리딩할 때는 리딩에만 집중하자!** 원서를 읽는 중간중간 모르는 단어가 나온다고 워크북을 바로 펼쳐 보거나, 곧바로 번역을 찾아보는 것은 크게 도움이 되지 않습니다. 모르는 단어나 이해되지 않는 문장들은 따로 가볍게 표시만 해 두고, 전체적인 맥락을 파악하며 속도감 있게 읽어 나가세요. 리딩을 할 때는 속도에 대한 긴장감을 잃지 않으면서 리딩에만 집중하는 것이 좋습니다. 모르는 단어와 문장은 리딩을 마친 후에 한꺼번에 정리하는 '리뷰' 시간을 통해 점검하는 시간을 가지면 됩니다. 리뷰를 할 때는 번역은 물론 단어장과 사전도 꼼꼼하게 확인하면서 어떤 이유에서 이해가 되지 않았는지 생각해 봅니다.

- **번역 활용은 이렇게!** 이해가 가지 않는 문장은 번역을 통해서 그 의미를 파악할 수 있습니다. 하지만 한국어와 영어는 정확히 1:1 대응이 되지 않기 때문에 번역을 활용하는 데에도 지혜가 필요합니다. 의역이 된 부분까지 억지로 의미를 대응해서 이해하려고 하기보다, 어떻게 그런 의미가 만들어진 것인지 추측하면서 번역은 참고 자료로 활용하는 것이 좋습니다.

- **듣기 훈련은 이렇게!** 리스닝 실력을 향상시키고 싶다면 오디오북을 적극적으로 활용해 보세요. 처음에는 오디오북을 틀어 놓고 눈으로 해당 내용을 따라 읽으면서 훈련을 하고, 이것이 익숙해지면 오디오북만 틀어 놓고 '귀를 통해' 책을 읽어 보세요. 눈으로 읽지 않은 책이라도 귀를 통해 이해할 수 있을 정도가

THE ZACK FILES

되면, 이후에 영어 듣기로 어려움을 겪는 일은 거의 없을 것입니다.

- **2~3번 반복해서 읽자!** 영어 초보자라면 처음부터 완벽하게 이해하려고 하는 것보다는 2~3회 반복해서 읽을 것을 추천합니다. 처음 원서를 읽을 때는 생소한 단어들과 스토리 때문에 내용 파악에 급급할 수밖에 없습니다. 하지만 일단 내용을 파악한 후에 다시 읽으면 문장 구조나 어휘의 활용에 더 집중하게 되고, 원서를 더 깊이 있게 읽을 수 있습니다. 그 과정에서 리딩 속도에 탄력이 붙고 리딩 실력 또한 더 확고히 다지게 됩니다.

- **'시리즈'로 꾸준히 읽자!** 한 작가의 책을 시리즈로 읽는 것 또한 영어 실력 향상에 큰 도움이 됩니다. 같은 등장인물이 다시 나오기 때문에 내용 파악이 더 수월할 뿐 아니라, 작가가 사용하는 어휘와 표현들도 반복되기 때문에 탁월한 복습 효과까지 얻을 수 있습니다. 롱테일북스의 『잭 파일스』 시리즈는 현재 6권, 총 31,441단어 분량이 출간되어 있습니다. 시리즈를 꾸준히 읽다 보면 영어 실력이 자연스럽게 향상될 것입니다.

원서 본문 구성

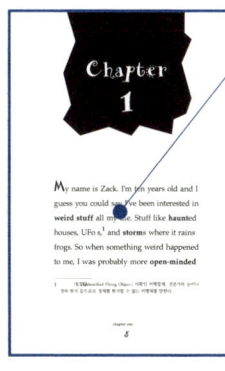

내용이 담긴 원서 본문입니다.

원어민이 읽는 일반 원서와 같은 텍스트지만, 암기해야 할 중요 어휘들은 볼드체로 표시되어 있습니다. 이 어휘들은 지금 들고 계신 워크북에 챕터별로 정리되어 있습니다.

학습 심리학 연구 결과에 따르면, 한 단어씩 따로 외우는 단어 암기는 거의 효과가 없다고 합니다. 단어를 제대로 외우기 위해서는 문맥(context) 속에서 단어를 암기해야 하며, 한 단어당 문맥 속에서 15번 이상 마주칠 때 완벽하게 암기할 수 있다고 합니다.

이 책의 본문에서는 중요 어휘를 볼드체로 강조하여, 문맥 속의 단어들을 더 확실히 인지(word cognition in context)하도록 돕고 있습니다. 또한 대부분의 중요 단어들은 다른 챕터에서도 반복해서 등장하기 때문에 이 책을 읽는 것만으로도 자연스럽게 어휘력을 향상시킬 수 있습니다.

본문 하단에는 내용 이해를 돕기 위한 '각주'가 첨가되어 있습니다. 각주는 굳이 암기할 필요는 없지만, 알아 두면 도움이 될 만한 정보를 설명하고 있습니다. 각주를 참고하면 스토리를 더 깊이 있게 이해할 수 있어 원서를 읽는 재미가 배가됩니다.

THE ZACK FILES

워크북(Workbook) 구성

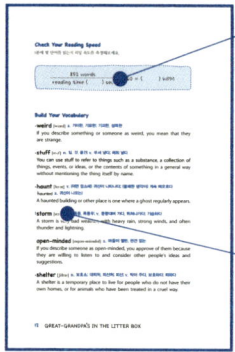

Check Your Reading Speed
해당 챕터의 단어 수가 기록되어 있어, 리딩 속도를 측정할 수 있습니다. 특히 리딩 속도를 중시하는 독자들이 유용하게 사용할 수 있습니다.

Build Your Vocabulary
본문에 볼드 표시되어 있는 단어들이 정리되어 있습니다. 리딩 전·후에 반복해서 보면 원서를 더욱 쉽게 읽을 수 있고, 어휘력도 빠르게 향상될 것입니다.

단어는 〈스펠링 – 빈도 – 발음기호 – 품사 – 한글 뜻 – 영문 뜻〉 순서로 표기되어 있으며 빈도 표시(★)가 많을수록 필수 어휘입니다. 반복해서 등장하는 단어는 빈도 대신 '복습'으로 표기되어 있습니다. 품사는 아래와 같이 표기했습니다.

n. 명사 | **a.** 형용사 | **ad.** 부사 | **v.** 동사
conj. 접속사 | **prep.** 전치사 | **int.** 감탄사 | **idiom** 숙어 및 관용구

Comprehension Quiz
간단한 퀴즈를 통해 읽은 내용에 대한 이해력을 점검해 볼 수 있습니다.

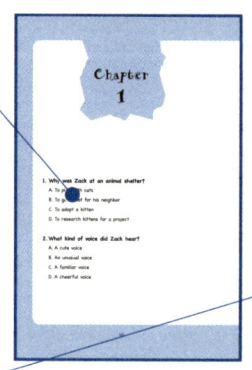

한국어 번역
영문과 비교할 수 있도록 최대한 직역에 가까운 번역을 담았습니다.

이 책의 수준과 타깃 독자

- **미국 원어민 기준:** 유치원 ~ 초등학교 저학년
- **한국 학습자 기준:** 초등학교 저학년 ~ 중학생
- 영어원서 완독 경험이 없는 초보 영어 학습자
- **비슷한 수준의 다른 챕터북:** Arthur Chapter Book,★ Flat Stanley,★ Tales from the Odyssey,★ Junie B. Jones,★ Magic Tree House, Marvin Redpost

★「롱테일 에디션」으로 출간된 도서

 QR 코드를 인식하여 「잭 파일스」 3권 원서 오디오북을 들어 보세요! 더불어 롱테일북스 홈페이지(www.longtailbooks.co.kr)에서도 오디오북 MP3 파일을 다운로드 받을 수 있습니다.

Chapter 1

1. **What did Zack think when the doors opened and closed one night?**
   A. He thought there was a logical explanation for it.
   B. He thought it was just part of a dream.
   C. He thought his dad was making the noise.
   D. He thought his whole apartment was being haunted.

2. **What was different about Zack's room when he woke up?**
   A. Some of his things were missing.
   B. His things were all over the place.
   C. Some of his things were dirty.
   D. His things looked more organized.

3. **Why did Zack clean up his room?**
   A. He liked keeping his room neat.
   B. He had not cleaned his room in a while.
   C. He did not have any other chores to do that morning.
   D. He did not want his dad to notice the mess.

4. **What happened when Zack got out of the bathroom?**
   A. He found a stranger in his room.
   B. He caught his dad trying to clean his room.
   C. He discovered his room was untidy again.
   D. He realized he had forgotten to put away some things in his room.

5. **What made Zack's dad finally believe Zack?**
   A. He saw all of Zack's belongings floating in the air.
   B. He heard someone moving all of Zack's belongings.
   C. He heard the TV turn on and off on its own.
   D. He saw the TV move on its own.

Check Your Reading Speed
1분에 몇 단어를 읽는지 리딩 속도를 측정해보세요.

$$\frac{745 \text{ words}}{\text{reading time ( ) sec}} \times 60 = (\quad) \text{ WPM}$$

Build Your Vocabulary

spooky [spúːki] a. 으스스한, 귀신이 나올 것 같은
If you say that something is spooky, you mean that it is strange or frightening in a way that makes you think of ghosts.

‡ realize [ríːəlàiz] v. 깨닫다, 알아차리다; 실현하다, 달성하다
If you realize that something is true, you become aware of that fact or understand it.

scary [skέəri] a. 무서운, 겁나는
Something that is scary is rather frightening.

★ weird [wiərd] a. 기이한, 기묘한; 기괴한, 섬뜩한
If you describe something or someone as weird, you mean that they are strange.

★ stuff [stʌf] n. 일, 것, 물건; v. 쑤셔 넣다; 채워 넣다
You can use stuff to refer to things such as a substance, a collection of things, events, or ideas, or the contents of something in a general way without mentioning the thing itself by name.

★ faucet [fɔ́ːsit] n. 수도꼭지
A faucet is a device that controls the flow of a liquid or gas from a pipe or container.

‡ blood [blʌd] n. 피, 혈액
Blood is the red liquid that flows inside your body, which you can see if you cut yourself.

‡ **honest** [ánist] a. 솔직한; 정직한 (to be honest idiom 솔직하게 말하면)
You can say 'to be honest' to indicate that you are telling the truth about your own opinions or feelings.

‡ **mention** [ménʃən] v. 말하다, 언급하다; n. 언급, 거론
If you mention something, you say something about it, usually briefly.

★ **closet** [klázit] n. 벽장, 붙박이장
A closet is a piece of furniture with doors at the front and shelves inside, which is used for storing things.

‡ **figure** [fígjər] v. 생각하다; 중요하다; n. 사람; 모습; 수치; (중요한) 인물
If you figure that something is the case, you think or guess that it is the case.

no big deal idiom 별일 아니다, 대수롭지 않다
You use 'no big deal' to say that something is not important or not a problem.

‡ **casual** [kǽʒuəl] a. 태평스러운, 무심한; 격식을 차리지 않는
If you are casual, you are, or you pretend to be, relaxed and not very concerned about what is happening or what you are doing.

‡ **notice** [nóutis] v. 알아채다, 인지하다; 주의하다; n. 신경 씀, 알아챔; 통지, 예고
If you notice something or someone, you become aware of them.

messy [mési] a. 지저분한, 엉망인; 골치 아픈
Something that is messy is dirty or untidy.

‡ **shade** [ʃeid] n. 빛 가리개; 그늘; 색조; v. 그늘지게 하다, 가리다
(window shade n. (창문의) 블라인드)
A shade is a piece of stiff cloth or heavy paper that you can pull down over a window as a covering.

★ **toss** [tɔːs] v. (가볍게) 던지다; (고개를) 홱 쳐들다; n. 던지기
If you toss something somewhere, you throw it there lightly, often in a rather careless way.

‡ waste [weist] n. 쓰레기; 낭비, 허비; v. 낭비하다; 헛되이 쓰다 (wastebasket n. 쓰레기통)
A wastebasket is a container for rubbish, especially paper, which is usually placed on the floor in the corner of a room or next to a desk.

‡ ceiling [síːliŋ] n. 천장
A ceiling is the horizontal surface that forms the top part or roof inside a room.

underpants [ʌ́ndərpæ̀nts] n. (남성용·여성용) 팬티
Underpants are a piece of underwear which have two holes to put your legs through and elastic around the top to hold them up round your waist or hips.

‡ imagine [imǽdʒin] v. 생각하다; 상상하다
If you imagine that something is the case, you think that it is the case.

‡ neat [niːt] a. 정돈된, 단정한; 깔끔한; 뛰어난 (neatness n. 정돈된 상태, 깔끔함)
A neat place, thing, or person is tidy and smart, and has everything in the correct place.

freak [friːk] n. ~에 광적으로 관심이 많은 사람; 괴짜; a. 아주 기이한; v. 기겁을 하다
If you describe someone as a particular kind of freak, you are emphasizing that they are very enthusiastic about a thing or activity, and often seem to think about nothing else.

‡ stand [stænd] v. 참다, 견디다; 서다; n. 관중석; 가판대
If you cannot stand something, you cannot bear it or tolerate it.

‡ brush [brʌʃ] v. 솔질을 하다; (솔이나 손으로) 털다; n. 붓; 솔; 비
(brush one's teeth idiom 이를 닦다)
If you brush something or brush something such as dirt off it, you clean it or tidy it using a brush.

goofy [gúːfi] a. 우스꽝스러운; 바보 같은, 얼빠진
If you describe someone or something as goofy, you think they are rather silly or ridiculous.

‡ **rub** [rʌb] v. 문지르다; (두 손 등을) 맞비비다; n. 문지르기, 비비기
If you rub a substance into a surface or rub something such as dirt from a surface, you spread it over the surface or remove it from the surface using your hand or something such as a cloth.

⋆ **toilet** [tɔ́ilit] n. 변기; 화장실
A toilet is a large bowl with a seat, or a platform with a hole, which is connected to a water system and which you use when you want to get rid of urine or feces from your body.

⋆ **sneak** [sniːk] v. 살금살금 가다; 몰래 하다; a. 기습적인
If you sneak somewhere, you go there very quietly on foot, trying to avoid being seen or heard.

prank [præŋk] n. (농담으로 하는) 장난
(play a prank on idiom ~에게 짓궂은 장난을 치다)
A prank is a trick, especially one which is played on someone to make them look silly.

hallway [hɔ́ːlwèi] n. 복도; 통로; 현관
A hallway in a building is a long passage with doors into rooms on both sides of it.

⋆ **mess** [mes] n. (지저분하고) 엉망인 상태; (많은 문제로) 엉망인 상황; v. 엉망으로 만들다
If you say that something is a mess or in a mess, you think that it is in an untidy state.

⋆ **electrical** [iléktrikəl] a. 전기의; 전기를 이용하는
Electrical systems or parts supply or use electricity.

⋆ **cord** [kɔːrd] n. 전선; 끈, 줄
Cord is wire covered in rubber or plastic which connects electrical equipment to an electricity supply.

‡ **tie** [tai] v. (매듭을 지어) 묶다, 매다; (끈 등으로) 묶다; n. 넥타이; 끈
If you tie a knot or bow in something or tie something in a knot or bow, you fasten the ends together.

bow [bou] ① n. 나비 모양 매듭; 활; ② v. 허리를 굽혀 인사하다; n. (고개 숙여 하는) 인사
A bow is a knot with two loops and two loose ends that is used in tying shoelaces and ribbons.

‡ **frame** [freim] v. 액자에 넣다; n. 틀, 액자; (건물·차량 등의) 뼈대
When a picture or photograph is framed, it is put in a frame.

* **moustache** [mʌ́stæʃ] n. (= mustache) 콧수염
A man's moustache is the hair that grows on his upper lip.

* **beard** [biərd] n. (턱)수염
A man's beard is the hair that grows on his chin and cheeks.

‡ **upset** [ʌpsét] a. 속상한, 마음이 상한; v. 속상하게 하다
If you are upset, you are unhappy or disappointed because something unpleasant has happened to you.

‡ **split** [split] v. (split-split) 헤어지다; 분열되다; 나뉘다; n. 분열; 분할
(split up idiom 헤어지다)
If two people split up, they end their relationship or marriage.

‡ **swear** [swεər] v. 맹세하다; 욕을 하다
If you say that you swear that something is true or that you can swear to it, you are saying very firmly that it is true.

* **haunt** [hɔ:nt] v. 귀신이 나타나다; (불쾌한 생각이) 계속 떠오르다
(haunted a. 귀신에 사로잡힌)
A ghost or spirit that haunts a place or a person regularly appears in the place, or is seen by the person and frightens them.

‡ **mind** [maind] v. 신경 쓰다, 상관하다; 조심하다; n. 마음, 정신
If someone does not mind what happens or what something is like, they do not have a strong preference for any particular thing.

‡ **careless** [kέərlis] a. 부주의한, 조심성이 없는; 경솔한
If you say that someone is careless of something such as their health or appearance, you mean that they do not seem to be concerned about it, or do nothing to keep it in a good condition.

fib [fib] v. (사소한) 거짓말을 하다; n. (사소한) 거짓말
If someone is fibbing, they are telling lies.

‡ buy [bai] v. 믿다; 사다
If you buy an idea or a theory, you believe and accept it.

★ precise [prisáis] a. 바로 그; 정확한, 정밀한; 꼼꼼한
You use precise to emphasize that you are referring to an exact thing, rather than something vague.

★ bookcase [búkkeis] n. 책장, 책꽂이
A bookcase is a piece of furniture with shelves that you keep books on.

‡ float [flout] v. (물 위나 공중에서) 떠가다; (물에) 뜨다; n. 부표
Something that floats in or through the air hangs in it or moves slowly and gently through it.

‡ land [lænd] v. (땅·표면에) 내려앉다; (비행기나 배로) 도착하다; n. 육지, 땅; 지역
When someone or something lands, they come down to the ground after moving through the air or falling.

dresser [drésər] n. 서랍장; 화장대
A dresser is a chest of drawers, usually with a mirror on the top.

after all idiom (예상과는 달리) 결국에는; 어쨌든
You use after all when you are saying that something that you thought might not be the case is in fact the case.

Chapter 2

1. **Why did Zack and his dad go into the kitchen?**

   A. To prepare breakfast

   B. To get away from Zack's room

   C. To check if anything strange was going on

   D. To trap the ghost in their apartment

2. **What was weird about the kitchen?**

   A. The table was broken.

   B. The cupboard doors were closed.

   C. The dishes were stacked up high.

   D. The refrigerator was swaying back and forth.

3. How did Zack describe poltergeists?
    A. They create chaos in people's homes.
    B. They do not realize they are in people's homes.
    C. They steal valuable items from people's homes.
    D. They live in the trash in people's homes.

4. What did Zack's dad suggest?
    A. Pretending there was nothing wrong
    B. Asking the ghost what it wanted
    C. Sleeping somewhere else that night
    D. Staying in the kitchen all day

5. What caused Zack to change his mind about the motel?
    A. There was nothing he wanted to eat at home.
    B. He figured it might be fun to stay there.
    C. His dad insisted on giving it a chance.
    D. The situation at home was out of control.

Check Your Reading Speed
1분에 몇 단어를 읽는지 리딩 속도를 측정해보세요.

$$\frac{255 \text{ words}}{\text{reading time ( ) sec}} \times 60 = (\quad) \text{ wPM}$$

Build Your Vocabulary

‡ block [blak] v. 막다, 차단하다; 방해하다; n. 구역, 블록; 사각형 덩어리
To block a road, channel, or pipe means to put an object across it or in it so that nothing can pass through it or along it.

stepladder [stéplædər] n. 발판 사다리
A stepladder is a portable ladder that is made of two sloping parts that are hinged together at the top so that it will stand up on its own.

yikes [jaiks] int. 이크, 으악 (놀랐을 때 내는 소리)
Yikes is used to show that you are worried, surprised, or shocked.

upside down [ʌpsaid dáun] ad. (아래위가) 거꾸로
If something has been moved upside down, it has been turned round so that the part that is usually lowest is above the part that is usually highest.

⋆ cupboard [kʌ́bərd] n. 식기장, 찬장
A cupboard is a piece of furniture that has one or two doors, usually contains shelves, and is used to store things.

‡ pile [pail] v. 쌓다; 집어넣다; 우르르 가다; n. 쌓아 놓은 것, 더미; 무더기
If you pile things somewhere, you put them there on top of each other.

⋆ stack [stæk] n. 무더기, 더미; v. (깔끔하게 정돈하여) 쌓다
A stack of things is a pile of them.

sway [swei] v. (전후·좌우로) 흔들리다; (마음을) 동요시키다; n. (전후·좌우로) 흔들림
When people or things sway, they lean or swing slowly from one side to the other.

unsteady [ənstédi] a. 불안정한; 비틀비틀하는 (unsteadily ad. 불안정하게)
Unsteady objects are not held, fixed, or balanced securely.

back and forth idiom 앞뒤로, 왔다 갔다
If someone moves back and forth, they repeatedly move in one direction and then in the opposite direction.

doubt [daut] n. 의심, 의혹, 의문; v. 확신하지 못하다, 의심하다, 의문을 갖다
If you have doubt or doubts about something, you feel uncertain about it and do not know whether it is true or possible.

stuff [stʌf] n. 일, 것, 물건; v. 쑤셔 넣다; 채워 넣다
You can use stuff to refer to things such as a substance, a collection of things, events, or ideas, or the contents of something in a general way without mentioning the thing itself by name.

in case idiom (~할) 경우에 대비해서
If you do something in case or just in case a particular thing happens, you do it because that thing might happen.

trash [træʃ] v. 엉망으로 만들다, 부수다; (필요 없는 것을) 버리다; n. 쓰레기
If someone trashes a place or vehicle, they deliberately destroy it or make it very dirty.

inn [in] n. 소규모 호텔, 여관
An inn is a small hotel or pub, usually an old one.

motel [moutél] n. 모텔, 자동차 여행자의 숙박소
A motel is a hotel intended for people who are traveling by car.

stove [stouv] n. (요리용 가스·전기) 레인지; 스토브, 난로
A stove is a piece of equipment which provides heat, either for cooking or for heating a room.

★ **flip** [flɪp] v. 홱 뒤집다, 휙 젖히다; 툭 던지다; n. 회전; 톡 던지기
If something flips over, or if you flip it over or into a different position, it moves or is moved into a different position.

복습 **land** [lænd] v. (땅·표면에) 내려앉다; (비행기나 배로) 도착하다; n. 육지, 땅; 지역
When someone or something lands, they come down to the ground after moving through the air or falling.

‡ **pan** [pæn] n. (= frying pan) 프라이팬; (얕은) 냄비
A frying pan is a flat metal pan with a long handle, in which you fry food.

teeter [tíːtər] v. (넘어질 듯이) 불안하게 서다; 흔들리다
If someone or something teeters, they shake in an unsteady way, and seem to be about to lose their balance and fall over.

★ **collapse** [kəlǽps] v. 붕괴되다, 무너지다; 쓰러지다; 실패하다; n. 실패; 붕괴; 쇠약
If a building or other structure collapses, it falls down very suddenly.

‡ **crash** [kræʃ] n. 요란한 소리; (자동차·항공기) 사고; v. 충돌하다; 부딪치다
A crash is a sudden, loud noise.

★ **smash** [smæʃ] v. 박살내다; (세게) 부딪치다; 부서지다; n. 박살내기; 요란한 소리
If you smash something or if it smashes, it breaks into many pieces, for example when it is hit or dropped.

★ **refrigerator** [rifrídʒərèitər] n. 냉장고
A refrigerator is a large container which is kept cool inside, usually by electricity, so that the food and drink in it stays fresh.

‡ **spring** [sprɪŋ] v. (sprang-sprung) 휙 움직이다; 튀다; n. 샘; 봄; 생기, 활기
If something springs in a particular direction, it moves suddenly and quickly.

★ **spill** [spɪl] v. 쏟아져 나오다; (액체를) 흘리다, 쏟다; n. 흘린 액체, 유출물
If the contents of a bag, box, or other container spill or are spilled, they come out of the container onto a surface.

on the other hand idiom 한편으로는, 반면에
You use on the other hand to introduce the second of two contrasting points, facts, or ways of looking at something.

Chapter 3

1. What happened at Zack's school?

    A. Zack could not find his homework.

    B. Zack slept through class.

    C. Zack wrote about his problem.

    D. Zack had trouble concentrating.

2. What did Mr. Hoffman ask Zack?

    A. He asked where Zack's home was.

    B. He asked if Zack was feeling ill.

    C. He asked why Zack was afraid of spirits.

    D. He asked what Zack was thinking about.

3. How did the other kids react when Zack mentioned the poltergeist?

   A. They seemed interested in hearing more.

   B. They did not take Zack seriously.

   C. They tried to hide their shock.

   D. They were concerned about Zack.

4. What was NOT true about Vernon?

   A. He had a lot of bad habits.

   B. He was well known in school.

   C. He felt embarrassed by his sweat.

   D. He was not nice to Zack.

5. What was Mr. Hoffman's advice?

   A. Zack should find out more information on poltergeists.

   B. Zack should not talk about superstitions in class.

   C. Zack should focus on his schoolwork in the library.

   D. Zack should stop believing in the supernatural.

Check Your Reading Speed
1분에 몇 단어를 읽는지 리딩 속도를 측정해보세요.

$$\frac{501 \text{ words}}{\text{reading time ( ) sec}} \times 60 = (\quad) \text{ wPM}$$

Build Your Vocabulary

tune out idiom ~을 듣지 않고 딴청을 부리다, 무시하다
If you tune out, you stop listening or paying attention to what is being said.

★ **startle** [stɑ:rtl] v. 깜짝 놀라게 하다; 움찔하다; n. 깜짝 놀람 (startled a. 깜짝 놀란)
If something sudden and unexpected startles you, it surprises and frightens you slightly.

‡ **opinion** [əpínjən] n. 의견, 견해, 생각
Your opinion about something is what you think or believe about it.

clear one's throat idiom 목을 가다듬다; 헛기침하다
If you clear your throat, you cough once in order to make it easier to speak or to attract people's attention.

★ **loosen** [lu:sn] v. 느슨하게 하다; 풀다; (통제·구속 등을) 완화하다
If you loosen your clothing or something that is tied or fastened or if it loosens, you undo it slightly so that it is less tight or less firmly held in place.

복습 **tie** [tai] n. 넥타이; 끈; v. (매듭을 지어) 묶다, 매다; (끈 등으로) 묶다
A tie is a long narrow piece of cloth that is worn round the neck under a shirt collar and tied in a knot at the front.

★ **stall** [stɔ:l] v. (고의로) 시간을 끌다; (차량·엔진이) 멈추다; n. 가판대
If you stall, you deliberately delay because you are not ready to do something, for example, answer questions.

‡ form [fɔːrm] v. 형성하다; 만들어 내다; n. 종류, 유형; 방식; 서식
If you form a relationship, a habit, or an idea, or if it forms, it begins to exist and develop.

‡ discuss [diskʌ́s] v. 의견을 나누다, 논하다; (말·글 등으로) 논하다 (discussion n. 논의)
If there is discussion about something, people talk about it, often in order to reach a decision.

복습 honest [ánist] a. 솔직한; 정직한
If you are honest in a particular situation, you tell the complete truth or give your sincere opinion, even if this is not very pleasant.

‡ spirit [spírit] n. 유령, 정령; 영혼; 기분, 마음; 태도
A spirit is a ghost or supernatural being.

★ invisible [invízəbl] a. 보이지 않는, 볼 수 없는
If you describe something as invisible, you mean that it cannot be seen, for example because it is transparent, hidden, or very small.

‡ force [fɔːrs] n. 힘; 폭력; 영향력; v. 억지로 ~하다; ~를 강요하다
Force is the power or strength which something has.

★ wreck [rek] v. 엉망으로 만들다; 파괴하다; n. 충돌; 사고 잔해
To wreck something means to completely destroy or ruin it.

★ superstitious [sùːpərstíʃəs] a. 미신을 믿는, 미신적인
People who are superstitious believe in things that are not real or possible, for example magic.

★ sweat [swet] v. 땀을 흘리다; 식은땀을 흘리다, 불안해하다; n. 땀; 노력, 수고
When you sweat, you produce liquid on the surface of your skin when you are hot, nervous, or ill.

brag [bræg] v. (심하게) 자랑하다
If you brag, you say in a very proud way that you have something or have done something.

‡ **gym** [dʒim] n. 운동; 체육관
Gym is the activity of doing physical exercises in a gym, especially at school.

‡ **grade** [greid] n. 학년; (상품의) 품질; 등급; v. (등급을) 나누다; 성적을 매기다
In the United States, a grade is a group of classes in which all the children are of a similar age.

* **legend** [lédʒənd] n. 전설적인 인물; 전설
If you refer to someone as a legend, you mean that they are very famous and admired by a lot of people.

* **fairy** [féəri] n. (이야기 속의) 요정
A fairy is an imaginary creature with magical powers. Fairies are often represented as small people with wings.

* **tolerate** [tálərèit] v. 용인하다; (불쾌한 일을) 참다; 견디다
If you tolerate a situation or person, you accept them although you do not particularly like them.

supernatural [suːpərnǽtʃərəl] n. 초자연적 현상; a. 초자연적인
Supernatural creatures, forces, and events are believed by some people to exist or happen, although they are impossible according to scientific laws.

‡ **suggest** [səgdʒést] v. (아이디어·계획을) 제안하다; 추천하다; 시사하다
If you suggest something, you put forward a plan or idea for someone to think about.

‡ **research** [rísəːrtʃ] n. 연구, 조사; v. 연구하다, 조사하다
Research is work that involves studying something and trying to discover facts about it.

‡ **solution** [səlúːʃən] n. (문제·곤경의) 해법, 해결책
A solution to a problem or difficult situation is a way of dealing with it so that the difficulty is removed.

come to think of it idiom 그러고 보니, 생각해 보니
You use 'come to think of it,' when you mention something that you have suddenly remembered or realized.

Chapter 4

1. **What kind of book did the librarian recommend?**
   A. A book on the history of black magic
   B. A book on using white magic
   C. A book on removing evil spirits
   D. A book on common spiritual traditions

2. **According to one book, what did Zack have to do?**
   A. He had to offer the poltergeist a gift.
   B. He had to approach the spirit gently.
   C. He had to light a candle seven times.
   D. He had to say a specific chant.

3. Why was Vernon in the library?
    A. He had a problem that was similar to Zack's.
    B. He wanted to apologize to Zack for teasing him.
    C. He was figuring out a way to help Zack.
    D. He hoped to impress Zack with his knowledge of ghosts.

4. What was happening to Vernon?
    A. His apartment was not as tidy as he expected it to be.
    B. He needed to clean his home more often than he wanted to.
    C. He was having a hard time finding his rearranged things.
    D. His room was being organized in a way that he disliked.

5. What was Zack thinking of doing later?
    A. Inviting Vernon to his home
    B. Helping Vernon with a banishing ritual
    C. Checking out more books with Vernon
    D. Becoming close friends with Vernon

Check Your Reading Speed
1분에 몇 단어를 읽는지 리딩 속도를 측정해보세요.

$$\frac{788 \text{ words}}{\text{reading time ( ) sec}} \times 60 = (\quad) \text{ wPM}$$

Build Your Vocabulary

‡ public [pʌ́blik] a. 공공의; 대중의; 공개되는; n. 일반 사람들, 대중
Public buildings and services are provided for everyone to use.

⋆ encyclopedia [insàikləpíːdiə] n. 백과사전
An encyclopedia is a book or set of books in which facts about many different subjects or about one particular subject are arranged for reference, usually in alphabetical order.

‡ stuff [stʌf] n. 일, 것, 물건; v. 쑤셔 넣다; 채워 넣다
You can use stuff to refer to things such as a substance, a collection of things, events, or ideas, or the contents of something in a general way without mentioning the thing itself by name.

get rid of idiom ~을 처리하다, 없애다
When you get rid of something that you do not want or do not like, you take action so that you no longer have it or suffer from it.

⋆ librarian [laibréəriən] n. (도서관의) 사서
A librarian is a person who is in charge of a library or who has been specially trained to work in a library.

‡ moustache [mʌ́stæʃ] n. (= mustache) 콧수염
A man's moustache is the hair that grows on his upper lip.

work out idiom 운동하다; ~을 계획해 내다; (일이) 잘 풀리다
If you work out, you do physical exercises in order to make your body fit and strong.

‡ **weight** [weit] n. 역기, 웨이트; 무게; 추; v. (추를 달아) 무겁게 하다
You can refer to a heavy object as a weight, especially when you have to lift it.

★ **reference** [réfərəns] n. 참고, 참조; 언급; v. 참고 표시를 하다
(reference book n. 참고 도서)
Reference books are ones that you look at when you need specific information or facts about a subject.

‡ **exact** [igzǽkt] a. 정확한; 꼼꼼한, 빈틈없는 (exactly ad. 정확히)
You use exactly before an amount, number, or position to emphasize that it is no more, no less, or no different from what you are stating.

★ **frown** [fraun] v. 얼굴을 찡그리다; 눈살을 찌푸리다; n. 찡그림, 찌푸림
When someone frowns, their eyebrows become drawn together, because they are annoyed, worried, or puzzled, or because they are concentrating.

put on idiom 놀리다; ~인 척하다
If you put someone on, you deceive them, often in a joking way.

cockroach [kákròuʧ] n. [곤충] 바퀴벌레
A cockroach is a large brown insect that is sometimes found in warm places or where food is kept.

★ **banish** [bǽniʃ] v. 제거하다, 사라지게 하다; 추방하다
If you banish something unpleasant, you get rid of it.

★ **ritual** [ríʧuəl] n. (종교적인) 의례; 의식과 같은 일
A ritual is a religious service or other ceremony which involves a series of actions performed in a fixed order.

roach [rouʧ] n. (= cockroach) [곤충] 바퀴벌레
A roach is the same as a cockroach which is a large brown insect.

‡ **motel** [moutél] n. 모텔, 자동차 여행자의 숙박소
A motel is a hotel intended for people who are traveling by car.

‡ **spirit** [spírit] n. 유령, 정령; 영혼; 기분, 마음; 태도
A spirit is a ghost or supernatural being.

stairway [stéərwei] n. (건물 내·외부에 있는) 계단
A stairway is a staircase or a flight of steps, inside or outside a building.

in case idiom (~할) 경우에 대비해서
If you do something in case or just in case a particular thing happens, you do it because that thing might happen.

bunny [bʌ́ni] n. [동물] 토끼
A bunny or a bunny rabbit is a child's word for a rabbit.

★**curse** [kə:rs] n. 저주; 욕설, 악담; v. 저주를 내리다; 욕설을 하다
If you say that there is a curse on someone, you mean that there seems to be a supernatural power causing unpleasant things to happen to them.

fool around idiom ~를 가지고 장난치다
If you fool around with something, you behave in a silly or dangerous way with them.

‡**evil** [íːvəl] a. 사악한, 악랄한; 유해한; 악마의; n. 악
If you describe someone as evil, you mean that they are very wicked by nature and take pleasure in doing things that harm other people.

be supposed to idiom ~해야 한다, ~하기로 되어 있다
If you say that something is supposed to happen, you mean that it is planned or expected.

demon [díːmən] n. 악령, 악마
A demon is an evil spirit.

★**dwell** [dwel] v. 살다, 거주하다
If you dwell somewhere, you live there.

filth [filθ] n. 오물, 쓰레기
Filth is a disgusting amount of dirt.

stink [stiŋk] v. (고약한) 냄새가 나다; 형편없다; n. 악취 (stinking a. 악취가 나는)
If you describe something as stinking, you mean that it has a very strong unpleasant smell.

cast out idiom 내쫓다, 쫓아 버리다
If you cast someone out, you get rid of them, especially by using force.

command [kəmǽnd] v. 명령하다, 지시하다; 지휘하다; n. 명령; 지휘, 통솔
If someone in authority commands you to do something, they tell you that you must do it.

depart [dipá:rt] v. 떠나다, 출발하다; 그만두다
When something or someone departs from a place, they leave it and start a journey to another place.

order [ɔ́:rdər] v. 명령을 내리다; 주문하다; n. 주문; 명령; 순서
If a person in authority orders someone to do something, they tell them to do it.

foul [faul] a. (날씨가) 사나운; (성격·맛 등이) 더러운, 아주 안 좋은
Foul weather is unpleasant, windy, and stormy.

upside down [ʌ́psàid dáun] a. (아래위가) 거꾸로 된
If something has been moved upside down, it has been turned round so that the part that is usually lowest is above the part that is usually highest.

inside out [insaid áut] a. (안팎을) 뒤집어 놓은
If something such as a piece of clothing is inside out, the part that is normally inside now faces outward.

rouse [rauz] v. (잠든 사람을) 깨우다; 분발하게 하다; (어떤 감정을) 불러일으키다
If someone rouses you when you are sleeping or if you rouse, you wake up.

immediate [imí:diət] a. 즉각적인; 당면한 (immediately ad. 즉시, 즉각)
If something happens immediately, it happens without any delay.

ancient [éinʃənt] a. 고대의; 아주 오래된
Ancient means belonging to the distant past, especially to the period in history before the end of the Roman Empire.

on the other hand idiom 한편으로는, 반면에
You use on the other hand to introduce the second of two contrasting points, facts, or ways of looking at something.

trash [træʃ] v. 엉망으로 만들다, 부수다; (필요 없는 것을) 버리다; n. 쓰레기
If someone trashes a place or vehicle, they deliberately destroy it or make it very dirty.

checkout [tʃékaut] n. (도서의) 대출, 대여; 계산대
The checkout is the action or an instance of borrowing a book from a library.

load [loud] n. (수·양이) 많음; (많은 양의) 짐; v. 싣다
If you refer to a load of people or things or loads of them, you are emphasizing that there are a lot of them.

sweat [swet] v. 땀을 흘리다; 식은땀을 흘리다, 불안해하다; n. 땀; 노력, 수고
When you sweat, you produce liquid on the surface of your skin when you are hot, nervous, or ill.

superstitious [sùːpərstíʃəs] a. 미신을 믿는, 미신적인
People who are superstitious believe in things that are not real or possible, for example magic.

bug out idiom (놀람·공포 등으로) 눈이 휘둥그레지다
If your eyes bug out, they suddenly open wide because you are surprised or excited.

pop [pap] v. 펑 터지다, 터뜨리다; 눈이 휘둥그레지다; n. 펑 (하는 소리)
If something such as a balloon pops, or if you pop it, it bursts and makes a sudden loud noise.

vein [vein] n. 혈관, 정맥; 특질; 방식
Your veins are the thin tubes in your body through which your blood flows toward your heart.

stammer [stǽmər] v. 말을 더듬다; n. 말 더듬기
If you stammer, you speak with difficulty, hesitating and repeating words or sounds.

★ **convince** [kənvíns] v. 설득하다; 납득시키다, 확신시키다 (convincing a. 설득력 있는)
If you describe someone or something as convincing, you mean that they make you believe that a particular thing is true, correct, or genuine.

check out idiom (책을) 대출하다; (호텔에서) 체크아웃하다; 확인하다, 조사하다
If you check out a book, you borrow it from a library.

‡ **nervous** [nə́ːrvəs] a. 불안해하는, 초조해하는; 신경의 (nervously ad. 불안하게)
If someone is nervous, they are frightened or worried about something that is happening or might happen, and show this in their behavior.

★ **whisper** [hwíspər] n. 속삭임, 소곤거리는 소리; v. 속삭이다, 소곤거리다
A whisper is a very quiet way of saying something so that other people cannot hear you.

weird [wiərd] a. 기이한, 기묘한; 기괴한, 섬뜩한
If you describe something or someone as weird, you mean that they are strange.

invisible [invízəbl] a. 보이지 않는, 볼 수 없는
If you describe something as invisible, you mean that it cannot be seen, for example because it is transparent, hidden, or very small.

force [fɔːrs] n. 힘; 폭력; 영향력; v. 억지로 ~하다; ~를 강요하다
Force is the power or strength which something has.

★ **amaze** [əméiz] v. (대단히) 놀라게 하다; 경악하게 하다 (amazed a. 놀란)
If something amazes you, it surprises you very much.

★ **straighten** [streitn] v. 똑바르게 하다; (자세를) 바로 하다
(straighten up idiom ~을 정리하다)
If you straighten up something, you make it tidy.

‡ **arrange** [əréindʒ] v. 배열하다, 정리하다; 마련하다, 처리하다 (rearrange v. 재배열하다)
If you rearrange things, you change the way in which they are organized or ordered.

make the bed idiom (침대를) 정리하다
If you make the bed, you arrange the sheets and blankets on it so someone can sleep there.

sheet [ʃiːt] n. 침대 시트, 얇은 천; (종이) 한 장
A sheet is a large rectangular piece of cotton or other cloth that you sleep on or cover yourself with in a bed.

blanket [blǽŋkit] n. 담요, 모포; v. (완전히) 뒤덮다
A blanket is a large square or rectangular piece of thick cloth, especially one which you put on a bed to keep you warm.

tuck [tʌk] v. (옷·시트의 자락을) 집어넣다; 끼워 넣다; n. 주름, 단
If you tuck something somewhere, you put it there so that it is safe, comfortable, or neat.

bounce [bauns] v. 튀기다, 튀다; 깡충깡충 뛰다; n. 튀어 오름; 탄력
When an object such as a ball bounces or when you bounce it, it moves upward from a surface or away from it immediately after hitting it.

check in with idiom ~에게 연락하다
If you check in with someone, you talk with them in order to report or find out new information.

neat [niːt] a. 정돈된, 단정한; 깔끔한; 뛰어난 (neatness n. 정돈된 상태, 깔끔함)
A neat place, thing, or person is tidy and smart, and has everything in the correct place.

be hot to idiom 열의에 차 있다
If you are hot to do something, you are very enthusiastic about doing it.

Chapter 5

1. What was the apartment like when Zack got home?

    A. It looked the same as before.

    B. There was something gooey everywhere.

    C. All the lights were turned on.

    D. Things were exploding into little pieces.

2. What did Wanda do with some M&Ms?

    A. She spelled words in another language.

    B. She made pictures on the ceiling.

    C. She responded to Zack's questions.

    D. She created riddles for Zack and his dad.

3. Why was Wanda messing up Zack's home?
    A. She had nothing else to do.
    B. She felt like punishing Zack.
    C. She wanted to get her home back.
    D. She was trying to be friendly.

4. What was true about Wanda?
    A. She died when she was an old woman.
    B. She missed living in Zack's apartment.
    C. She had been a spirit for only a few years.
    D. She did not have friends when she was alive.

5. What did Zack do after Wanda broke his Game Boy?
    A. He threatened to catch her.
    B. He accused her of always being bad.
    C. He claimed that she was jealous of him.
    D. He yelled that he would never forgive her.

Check Your Reading Speed
1분에 몇 단어를 읽는지 리딩 속도를 측정해보세요.

$$\frac{977 \text{ words}}{\text{reading time ( ) sec}} \times 60 = (\quad) \text{ wPM}$$

Build Your Vocabulary

freak [friːk] v. 기겁을 하다; n. ~에 광적으로 관심이 많은 사람; 괴짜; a. 아주 기이한 (freak out idiom 겁에 질리다)
If someone freaks out, or if something freaks them out, they suddenly feel extremely surprised, upset, angry, or confused.

complete [kəmplíːt] a. 가능한 최대의, 완벽한; v. 끝마치다 (completely ad. 완전히)
You use complete to emphasize that something is as great in extent, degree, or amount as it possibly can be.

gooey [guːi] a. 끈적끈적한, 들러붙는
If you describe a food or other substance as gooey, you mean that it is very soft and sticky.

combine [kəmbáin] v. 결합하다; 갖추다; 병행하다 (combination n. 조합, 결합)
A combination of things is a mixture of them.

rubber [rʌ́bər] n. 고무; a. 고무의
Rubber is a strong, waterproof, elastic substance made from the juice of a tropical tree or produced chemically.

croak [krouk] v. 목이 쉰 듯 말하다; (개구리나 까마귀가) 까악까악 울다; n. 꺽꺽하는 소리
If someone croaks something, they say it in a low, rough voice.

upset [ʌpsét] a. 속상한, 마음이 상한; v. 속상하게 하다
If you are upset, you are unhappy or disappointed because something unpleasant has happened to you.

★ **barely** [béərli] ad. 간신히, 가까스로; 거의 ~아니게
You use barely to say that something is only just true or only just the case.

‡ **horrible** [hɔ́:rəbl] a. 끔찍한, 지긋지긋한; 소름끼치는, 무시무시한; 못된
You can call something horrible when it causes you to feel great shock, fear, and disgust.

glassy [glǽsi] a. (눈이) 멀건; 무표정한; 유리 같은
If you describe someone's eyes or expression as glassy, you mean that they are showing no feeling, emotion, or awareness.

shell-shocked [ʃél-ʃàkt] a. 어쩔 줄 모르는
If you say that someone is shell-shocked, you mean that they are very shocked, usually because something bad has happened.

wobbly [wábli] a. (불안정하게) 흔들리는, 기우뚱한; 떨리는
If you feel wobbly or if your legs feel wobbly, you feel weak and have difficulty standing up, especially because you are afraid, ill, or exhausted.

‡ **charge** [ʧɑːrdʒ] n. 책임, 담당; 요금; v. (요금·값을) 청구하다
(take charge idiom 책임을 지다)
If you take charge of someone or something, you make yourself responsible for them and take control over them.

복습 **banish** [bǽniʃ] v. 제거하다; 사라지게 하다; 추방하다
If you banish something unpleasant, you get rid of it.

복습 **ritual** [ríʧuəl] n. (종교적인) 의례; 의식과 같은 일
A ritual is a religious service or other ceremony which involves a series of actions performed in a fixed order.

‡ **nod** [nad] v. (고개를) 끄덕이다, 까딱하다; n. (고개를) 끄덕임
If you nod, you move your head downward and upward to show that you are answering 'yes' to a question, or to show agreement, understanding, or approval.

★ **stare** [stɛər] v. 빤히 쳐다보다, 응시하다; n. 빤히 쳐다보기, 응시
If you stare at someone or something, you look at them for a long time.

‡ **confident** [kánfədənt] a. 자신감 있는; 확신하는
If a person or their manner is confident, they feel sure about their own abilities, qualities, or ideas.

복습 **evil** [íːvəl] a. 사악한, 악랄한; 유해한; 악마의; n. 악
If you describe someone as evil, you mean that they are very wicked by nature and take pleasure in doing things that harm other people.

복습 **demon** [díːmən] n. 악령, 악마
A demon is an evil spirit.

복습 **dwell** [dwel] v. 살다, 거주하다
If you dwell somewhere, you live there.

복습 **filth** [filθ] n. 오물, 쓰레기
Filth is a disgusting amount of dirt.

복습 **stink** [stiŋk] v. (고약한) 냄새가 나다; 형편없다; n. 악취 (stinking a. 악취가 나는)
If you describe something as stinking, you mean that it has a very strong unpleasant smell.

go on idiom 말을 계속하다; (어떤 상황이) 계속되다; 자자, 어서
To go on means to continue speaking after a short pause.

★ **slam** [slæm] v. 세게 치다, 놓다; 탁 닫다; n. 쾅 하고 닫기
If you slam something down, you put it there quickly and with great force.

‡ **shelf** [ʃelf] n. 선반; (책장의) 칸
A shelf is a flat piece of wood, metal, or glass which is attached to a wall or to the sides of a cupboard.

★ **explode** [iksplóud] v. 폭발하다; 갑자기 ~하다; 굉음을 내다
If an object such as a bomb explodes or if someone or something explodes it, it bursts loudly and with great force, often causing damage or injury.

ceiling [síːliŋ] n. 천장
A ceiling is the horizontal surface that forms the top part or roof inside a room.

spell [spel] v. (문자들이 어떤 단어를) 만들다; 철자를 맞게 쓰다; n. 주문; 마법
When you spell out a word, you write or speak each letter in the word in the correct order.

contact [kántækt] n. 연락, 접촉; v. 연락하다
(make contact with idiom ~와 접촉하다)
If you make contact with someone, you find out where they are and talk or write to them.

scare [skɛər] v. 놀라게 하다; 무서워하다; n. 불안(감); 놀람, 공포 (scared a. 무서워하는)
If you are scared of someone or something, you are frightened of them.

chill [ʧil] n. 오싹한 느낌; 냉기, 한기; v. 아주 춥게 하다; 오싹하게 하다
If something sends a chill through you, it gives you a sudden feeling of fear or anxiety.

freezer [fríːzər] n. 냉동고
A freezer is a large container like a fridge in which the temperature is kept below freezing point so that you can store food inside it for long periods.

freeze [friːz] v. (froze-frozen) 얼다; (두려움 등으로 몸이) 얼어붙다; n. 동결; 한파
(frozen a. 냉동된)
Frozen food has been preserved by being kept at a very low temperature.

tingle [tiŋgl] v. 따끔거리다; (어떤 감정이) 마구 일다; n. 따끔거림; 흥분
When a part of your body tingles, you have a slight stinging feeling there.

whisper [hwíspər] v. 속삭이다, 소곤거리다; n. 속삭임, 소곤거리는 소리
When you whisper, you say something very quietly, using your breath rather than your throat, so that only one person can hear you.

shaky [ʃéiki] a. 떨리는, 휘청거리는; 불안한
If your body or your voice is shaky, you cannot control it properly and it shakes, for example because you are ill or nervous.

daze [deiz] v. 멍하게 하다; 눈부시게 하다; n. 멍한 상태; 눈이 부심 (dazed a. 멍한)
If someone is dazed, they are confused and unable to think clearly, often because of shock or a blow to the head.

★ **respectful** [rispéktfəl] a. 공손한, 정중한; 경의를 표하는
If you are respectful, you show respect for someone.

★ **tone** [toun] n. 어조, 말투; 음색; (글의) 분위기; 색조
Someone's tone is a quality in their voice which shows what they are feeling or thinking.

★ **scrape** [skreip] v. 긁는 소리를 내다; 긁다; 긁어내다; n. 긁기; 긁힌 상처
If something scrapes against something else or if someone or something scrapes something else, it rubs against it, making a noise or causing slight damage.

복습 **arrange** [əréindʒ] v. 배열하다, 정리하다; 마련하다; 처리하다 (rearrange v. 재배열하다)
If you rearrange things, you change the way in which they are organized or ordered.

‡ **conversation** [kànvərséiʃən] n. 대화
If you have a conversation with someone, you talk with them, usually in an informal situation.

★ **scratch** [skrætʃ] v. 긁히는 소리를 내다; (가려운 데를) 긁다; n. 긁는 소리, 긁힌 자국
If something scratches against something else, it rubs a hard surface with a sharp object, often making a noise.

‡ **frank** [fræŋk] a. (불편할 정도로) 솔직한, 노골적인 (frankly ad. 솔직히 말하면)
You use frankly when you are expressing an opinion or feeling to emphasize that you mean what you are saying, especially when the person you are speaking to may not like it.

‡ **ruin** [ruːin] v. 엉망으로 만들다; 폐허로 만들다; n. 붕괴, 몰락; 파멸
To ruin something means to severely harm, damage, or spoil it.

‡ **furniture** [fəːrniʧər] n. 가구
Furniture consists of large objects such as tables, chairs, or beds that are used in a room for sitting or lying on or for putting things on or in.

keep up idiom ~을 계속하다; (~의 속도 등을) 따라가다
If you keep something up, you continue to do it or provide it.

mess [mes] n. (지저분하고) 엉망인 상태; (많은 문제로) 엉망인 상황; v. 엉망으로 만들다
If you say that something is a mess or in a mess, you think that it is in an untidy state.

make sense idiom 이해할 만하다, 말이 되다; 이해가 되다
If something makes sense, you can understand it.

sail [seil] v. 미끄러지듯 나아가다; 항해하다; n. 돛
If a person or thing sails somewhere, they move there smoothly and fairly quickly.

smash [smæʃ] v. (세게) 부딪치다; 부서지다; 박살내다; n. 박살내기; 요란한 소리
If something smashes or is smashed against something solid, it moves very fast and with great force against it.

teen [tiːn] a. (= teenage) 10대의; n. (= teenager) 청소년
Teen or teenage children are aged between thirteen and nineteen years old.

master [mǽstər] n. 대가, 명수; 주인; v. 숙달하다; a. 가장 중요한
If you say that someone is a master of a particular activity, you mean that they are extremely skilled at it.

galaxy [gǽləksi] n. [천문] 은하계; 은하수
A galaxy is an extremely large group of stars and planets that extends over many billions of light years.

wreck [rek] v. 엉망으로 만들다; 파괴하다; n. 충돌; 사고 잔해
To wreck something means to completely destroy or ruin it.

jerk [dʒəːrk] n. 얼간이; 홱 움직임; v. 홱 움직이다
If you call someone a jerk, you are insulting them because you think they are stupid or you do not like them.

troublemaker [trʌ́blmèikər] n. 말썽꾸러기
If you refer to someone as a troublemaker, you mean that they cause unpleasantness, quarrels, or fights.

afterlife [ǽftərlàif] n. 내세, 사후 세계
The afterlife is a life that some people believe begins when you die, for example a life in heaven or as another person or animal.

Chapter 6

1. **What did Zack's dad want to do?**
   A. Convince Wanda that she was being unfair
   B. Help Wanda become a living kid again
   C. Find a way to make Wanda happy
   D. Make Wanda and Zack be best friends

2. **Why didn't Zack want to play with Wanda?**
   A. He did not like playing with younger kids.
   B. He did not like spending time with girls.
   C. He did not want to play with a mean kid.
   D. He did not want to share his toys with anyone.

3. At first, why didn't Zack and his dad believe Wanda could fix their apartment?

   A. They figured she was not powerful enough.

   B. They thought she was too selfish to do anything nice.

   C. They believed it would take too much time.

   D. They assumed their apartment was too damaged.

4. What did Zack offer to do?

   A. Hang out with Wanda for one day

   B. Find someone for Wanda to play with

   C. Make up a fun game for Wanda to try

   D. Get Wanda out of the spirit world

5. What did Wanda do to the things in the apartment?

   A. She put them back in their original spots.

   B. She replaced them with new things.

   C. She glued them back together.

   D. She arranged them in a completely new order.

Check Your Reading Speed
1분에 몇 단어를 읽는지 리딩 속도를 측정해보세요.

$$\frac{684 \text{ words}}{\text{reading time ( ) sec}} \times 60 = (\quad) \text{ wPM}$$

Build Your Vocabulary

‡ cross [krɔːs] v. 서로 겹치게 놓다; (가로질러) 건너다; 교차하다; n. 십자 기호
(cross one's arms idiom 팔짱을 끼다)
If you cross your arms, legs, or fingers, you put one of them on top of the other.

‡ calm [kɑːm] a. 침착한, 차분한; 잔잔한; v. 진정시키다; n. 평온; 침착함
A calm person does not show or feel any worry, anger, or excitement.

복습 trash [træʃ] v. 엉망으로 만들다, 부수다; (필요 없는 것을) 버리다; n. 쓰레기
If someone trashes a place or vehicle, they deliberately destroy it or make it very dirty.

복습 go on idiom 말을 계속하다; (어떤 상황이) 계속되다; 자자, 어서
To go on means to continue speaking after a short pause.

★ yell [jel] v. 고함치다, 소리 지르다; n. 고함, 외침
If you yell, you shout loudly, usually because you are excited, angry, or in pain.

‡ helpful [hélpfəl] a. 도움이 되는; 기꺼이 돕는
Something that is helpful makes a situation more pleasant or more easy to tolerate.

point out idiom 지적하다, 언급하다; 알려주다
If you point out a fact or circumstance, you mention it in order to give someone information about it or make them notice it.

ceiling [síːliŋ] n. 천장
A ceiling is the horizontal surface that forms the top part or roof inside a room.

amaze [əméiz] v. (대단히) 놀라게 하다; 경악하게 하다 (amazed a. 놀란)
If something amazes you, it surprises you very much.

destroy [distrɔ́i] v. 파괴하다
To destroy something means to cause so much damage to it that it is completely ruined or does not exist any more.

wreck [rek] v. 엉망으로 만들다; 파괴하다; n. 충돌; 사고 잔해
To wreck something means to completely destroy or ruin it.

nuts [nʌts] a. 미친, 제정신이 아닌
If you say that someone goes nuts or is nuts, you mean that they go crazy or are very foolish.

treat [triːt] v. (특정한 태도로) 대하다; 여기다, 치부하다; n. 대접, 한턱
If you treat someone or something in a particular way, you behave toward them or deal with them in that way.

stuff [stʌf] n. 일, 것, 물건; v. 쑤셔 넣다; 채워 넣다
You can use stuff to refer to things such as a substance, a collection of things, events, or ideas, or the contents of something in a general way without mentioning the thing itself by name.

shift [ʃift] v. 조금 움직이다; (장소를) 옮기다; 바꾸다; n. 변화; 교대 근무 (시간)
If you shift something or if it shifts, it moves slightly.

combine [kəmbáin] v. 결합하다; 갖추다; 병행하다 (combination n. 조합, 결합)
A combination of things is a mixture of them.

war zone [wɔ́ːr zòun] n. 전쟁터, 교전 지역
A war zone is an area where a war is taking place or there is some other violent conflict.

★ **bet** [bet] v. 내기하다; (~이) 틀림없다; n. 짐작, 추측; 내기
If you bet on the result of a horse race, football game, or other event, you give someone a sum of money which they give you back with extra money if the result is what you predicted, or which they keep if it is not.

복습 **tingle** [tiŋgl] v. 따끔거리다; (어떤 감정이) 마구 일다; n. 따끔거림; 흥분
(tingly a. 따끔거리는)
If something makes your body feel tingly, it gives you a slight stinging feeling.

disintegrate [disíntəgrèit] v. 산산조각 나다; 붕괴되다
If an object or substance disintegrates, it breaks into many small pieces or parts and is destroyed.

‡ **blind** [blaind] v. (잠시) 안 보이게 하다; a. 눈이 먼; n. (창문에 치는) 블라인드
(blinding a. 눈이 부신)
A blinding light is extremely bright.

‡ **flash** [flæʃ] n. (잠깐) 반짝임; 순간; v. (잠깐) 번쩍이다; 휙 나타나다
A flash is a sudden burst of light or of something shiny or bright.

‡ **commercial** [kəmə́ːrʃəl] n. (텔레비전·라디오의) 광고; a. 상업의; 상업적인
A commercial is an advertisement that is broadcast on television or radio.

‡ **run** [rʌn] v. (필름 등을) 돌리다, 재생시키다; 운영하다; 달리다; n. 달리기; 연속
When you run a cassette or video tape or when it runs, it moves through the machine as the machine operates.

★ **reverse** [rivə́ːrs] n. (정)반대; (자동차의) 후진 기어; a. 반대의; v. 후진하다; 뒤바꾸다
(in reverse idiom 반대로)
If something happens in reverse, things happen in the opposite way to what usually happens or to what has been happening.

‡ **pool** [puːl] n. 수영장; 웅덩이; v. (자금·정보 등을) 모으다; 고이다
A pool is the same as a swimming pool which is a large hole in the ground that has been made and filled with water so that people can swim in it.

dive [daiv] v. (물속으로) 뛰어들다; 잠수하다; n. (물속으로) 뛰어들기; 잠수
(diving board n. 다이빙대)
A diving board is a board high above a swimming pool from which people can dive into the water.

trade [treid] n. 거래, 교역, 무역; v. 주고받다, 교환하다; 거래하다
(trick of the trade idiom 비법)
The tricks of the trade are the quick and clever ways of doing something that are known by people who regularly do a particular activity.

hopeful [hóupfəl] a. 희망에 찬, 기대하는; 희망적인
A hopeful action is one that you do in the hope that you will get what you want to get.

depend [dipénd] v. ~에 좌우되다, 달려 있다; 의존하다, 의지하다
You use depend in expressions such as it depends to indicate that you cannot give a clear answer to a question because the answer will be affected or determined by other factors.

shrug [ʃrʌg] v. (어깨를) 으쓱하다; n. 어깨를 으쓱하기
If you shrug, you raise your shoulders to show that you are not interested in something or that you do not know or care about something.

hang out with idiom ~와 어울려 놀다, 시간을 보내다
If you hang out with someone, you spend a lot of time with them.

exact [igzǽkt] a. 정확한; 꼼꼼한, 빈틈없는 (not exactly ad. 전혀 ~이 아닌)
You can use not exactly to show that you mean the opposite of what you are saying.

and all idiom ~을 포함하여
You use and all when you want to emphasize that what you are talking about includes the thing mentioned, especially when this is surprising or unusual.

playmate [pléimeit] n. (아이의) 놀이친구
A child's playmate is another child who often plays with him or her.

spirit [spírit] n. 유령, 정령; 영혼; 기분, 마음; 태도
A spirit is a ghost or supernatural being.

shudder [ʃʌ́dər] v. 마구 흔들리다; 몸을 떨다; n. 몸이 떨림, 전율; 크게 흔들림
If something such as a machine or vehicle shudders, it shakes suddenly and violently.

major [méidʒər] a. 큰; 주요한; 중요한; 심각한; n. 전공
You use major when you want to describe something that is more important, serious, or significant than other things in a group or situation.

earthquake [ə́:rθkweik] n. 지진
An earthquake is a shaking of the ground caused by movement of the earth's outer layer.

be about to idiom 막 ~하려는 참이다
If you are about to do something, you are going to do it immediately.

haze [heiz] n. 연무, 실안개; (정신이) 몽롱한 상태; v. 흐릿해지다 (hazy a. 희뿌연, 흐린)
Hazy weather conditions are those in which things are difficult to see, because of light mist, hot air, or dust.

sandstorm [sǽndstɔ:rm] n. (사막의) 모래 폭풍
A sandstorm is a strong wind in a desert area, which carries sand through the air.

silverware [sílvərwèr] n. 은제품, 은식기류
You can use silverware to refer to all the things in a house that are made of silver, especially the cutlery and dishes.

plate [pleit] n. 접시, 그릇; (자동차) 번호판; 판
A plate is a round or oval flat dish that is used to hold food.

pan [pæn] n. (얕은) 냄비; 프라이팬
A pan is a round metal container with a long handle, which is used for cooking things in, usually on top of a cooker or stove.

horrid [hɔ́:rid] a. 무시무시한; 매우 불쾌한, 지겨운
If you describe something as horrid, you mean that it is very unpleasant indeed.

scrape [skreip] v. 긁는 소리를 내다; 긁다; 긁어내다; n. 긁기; 긁힌 상처
If something scrapes against something else or if someone or something scrapes something else, it rubs against it, making a noise or causing slight damage.

grind [graind] v. (듣기 싫은 소리가 나게) 삐걱거리다; 갈다; 빻다
To grind means to make a harsh noise caused by rubbing things.

clang [klæŋ] v. 쨍그랑 하는 소리를 내다; n. 땡그랑, 쨍그랑
When a large metal object clangs, it makes a loud noise.

bounce [bauns] v. 튀기다, 튀다; 깡충깡충 뛰다; n. 튀어 오름; 탄력
When an object such as a ball bounces or when you bounce it, it moves upward from a surface or away from it immediately after hitting it.

glob [glab] n. 방울
A glob of something soft or liquid is a small round amount of it.

land [lænd] v. (땅·표면에) 내려앉다; (비행기나 배로) 도착하다; n. 육지, 땅; 지역
When someone or something lands, they come down to the ground after moving through the air or falling.

cheek [tʃi:k] n. 뺨, 볼; 엉덩이
Your cheeks are the sides of your face below your eyes.

saucer [sɔ́:sər] n. (컵 등의) 받침 접시
A saucer is a small curved plate on which you stand a cup.

come to think of it idiom 그러고 보니, 생각해 보니
You use 'come to think of it,' when you mention something that you have suddenly remembered or realized.

lift [lift] v. (안개가) 걷히다, 사라지다; 들어 올리다, 올라가다; n. (차 등을) 태워 주기
If fog, cloud, or mist lifts, it reduces, for example by moving upward or by becoming less thick.

CHAPTER 6 **57**

believe one's eyes idiom 본 것을 정말이라고 믿다
If you say that you cannot believe your eyes, you are emphasizing that you are very surprised about something you have seen.

gooey [guːi] a. 끈적끈적한, 들러붙는
If you describe a food or other substance as gooey, you mean that it is very soft and sticky.

complete [kəmpliːt] a. 가능한 최대의, 완벽한; v. 끝마치다 (completely ad. 완전히)
You use complete to emphasize that something is as great in extent, degree, or amount as it possibly can be.

neat [niːt] a. 정돈된, 단정한; 깔끔한; 뛰어난
A neat place, thing, or person is tidy and smart, and has everything in the correct place.

certain [səːrtn] a. 확실한, 틀림없는 (certainly ad. 틀림없이, 분명히)
If you are certain about something, you firmly believe it is true and have no doubt about it.

messy [mési] a. 지저분한, 엉망인; 골치 아픈
Something that is messy is dirty or untidy.

lottery [látəri] n. 복권, 추첨
A lottery is a type of gambling game in which people buy numbered tickets. Several numbers are then chosen, and the people who have those numbers on their tickets win a prize.

Chapter 7

1. What did Zack do as he walked to Vernon's apartment?
   A. He talked to random people on the street.
   B. He avoided passing people on the street.
   C. He whispered to Wanda so that no one could hear him.
   D. He spoke to Wanda even though people could hear him.

2. How did Wanda let Zack know she was still with him?
   A. She rearranged letters on street signs.
   B. She grabbed Zack's hat and pulled it down.
   C. She did strange things to other people.
   D. She set objects nearby on fire.

3. What was happening in Vernon's home when Zack arrived?

   A. Things were being reorganized and tidied up.
   B. Magazines were being delivered and piled up.
   C. Furniture was being covered with blankets.
   D. Dust was being moved to the front door.

4. What was true about Cecil?

   A. He had poor handwriting.
   B. He had a shy personality.
   C. He was both silly and energetic.
   D. He was both polite and clean.

5. How did Wanda communicate with Cecil?

   A. By using alphabet soup letters
   B. By making words with cereal
   C. By writing on a piece of paper
   D. By drawing pictures with a pen

Check Your Reading Speed
1분에 몇 단어를 읽는지 리딩 속도를 측정해보세요.

$$\frac{672 \text{ words}}{\text{reading time ( ) sec}} \times 60 = (\quad) \text{ wPM}$$

Build Your Vocabulary

★ **thrill** [θril] v. 정말 신나게 하다, 열광시키다; n. 흥분, 설렘; 전율 (thrilled a. 정말 신이 난)
If someone is thrilled, they are extremely pleased about something.

복습 **block** [blak] n. 구역, 블록; 사각형 덩어리; v. 막다, 차단하다; 방해하다
A block in a town is an area of land with streets on all its sides.

복습 **cross** [krɔːs] v. (가로질러) 건너다; 서로 겹치게 놓다; 교차하다; n. 십자 기호
If you cross something such as a room, a road, or an area of land or water, you move or travel to the other side of it.

★ **cuckoo** [kúːkuː] a. 미친; n. [동물] 뻐꾸기
If you say that someone is cuckoo, you mean that they are crazy.

‡ **sign** [sain] n. 신호, 몸짓; 표지판; 기색, 흔적; v. 서명하다; 신호를 보내다
A sign is a movement of your arms, hands, or head which is intended to have a particular meaning.

stuffy [stʌ́fi] a. 딱딱한, 격식적인; (건물·방 등이) 답답한
Stuffy people or institutions are formal and old-fashioned.

★ **straw** [strɔː] n. 짚, 밀짚; 빨대 (straw hat n. 밀짚모자)
Straw consists of the dried, yellowish stalks from crops such as wheat or barley.

★ **brim** [brim] n. (모자의) 챙; (컵·사발 등의) 위 끝부분; v. 그득하다; 그득 채우다
The brim of a hat is the wide part that sticks outward at the bottom.

all of a sudden idiom 갑자기
If something happens all of a sudden, it happens quickly and unexpectedly.

★**grab** [græb] v. (와락·단단히) 붙잡다; 급히 ~하다; n. 와락 잡아채려고 함
If you grab something, you take it or pick it up suddenly and roughly.

yank [jæŋk] v. 홱 잡아당기다; n. 홱 잡아당기기
If you yank someone or something somewhere, you pull them there suddenly and with a lot of force.

복습**stink** [stiŋk] v. (고약한) 냄새가 나다; 형편없다; n. 악취 (stinking a. 악취가 나는)
If you describe something as stinking, you mean that it has a very strong unpleasant smell.

복습**explode** [iksplóud] v. 폭발하다; 갑자기 ~하다; 굉음을 내다
If an object such as a bomb explodes or if someone or something explodes it, it bursts loudly and with great force, often causing damage or injury.

★**shower** [ʃáuər] n. 쏟아짐; 샤워; 소나기; v. (작은 조각들을) 쏟아 붓다; 샤워를 하다
You can refer to a lot of things that are falling as a shower of them.

★**spark** [spaːrk] n. 불꽃, 불똥; (전류의) 스파크; v. 불꽃을 일으키다; 촉발시키다
A spark is a tiny bright piece of burning material that flies up from something that is burning.

‡**cover** [kʌ́vər] v. 덮다; 씌우다, 가리다; n. 덮개; 위장; 몸을 숨길 곳
To cover something with or in something else means to put a layer of the second thing over its surface.

soot [sut] n. 그을음, 검댕
Soot is black powder which rises in the smoke from a fire and collects on the inside of chimneys.

‡**folk** [fouk] n. (pl.) 부모, 가족; 사람들; 여러분; a. 민속의, 전통적인
You can refer to your close family, especially your mother and father, as your folks.

CHAPTER 7 **63**

furniture [fə́:rniʃər] n. 가구
Furniture consists of large objects such as tables, chairs, or beds that are used in a room for sitting or lying on or for putting things on or in.

sweat [swet] v. 땀을 흘리다; 식은땀을 흘리다, 불안해하다; n. 땀; 노력, 수고
When you sweat, you produce liquid on the surface of your skin when you are hot, nervous, or ill.

neat [ni:t] a. 정돈된, 단정한; 깔끔한; 뛰어난
A neat place, thing, or person is tidy and smart, and has everything in the correct place.

arrange [əréindʒ] v. 배열하다, 정리하다; 마련하다, 처리하다 (rearrange v. 재배열하다)
If you rearrange things, you change the way in which they are organized or ordered.

dust [dʌst] n. 먼지, 티끌; v. 먼지를 털다; (고운 가루를) 뿌리다
Dust is the very small pieces of dirt which you find inside buildings, for example on furniture, floors, or lights.

rag [ræg] n. (걸레·행주로 쓰는) 낡은 헝겊, 해진 천
A rag is a piece of old cloth which you can use to clean or wipe things.

polish [páliʃ] v. (윤이 나도록) 닦다, 광을 내다; 손질하다; n. 광택제; 윤 내기
If you polish something, you put polish on it or rub it with a cloth to make it shine.

fancy [fǽnsi] a. 고급의; 복잡한; 장식이 많은; v. 생각하다, 상상하다
If you describe something as fancy, you mean that it is very expensive or of very high quality, and you often dislike it because of this.

stuff [stʌf] n. 일, 것, 물건; v. 쑤셔 넣다; 채워 넣다
You can use stuff to refer to things such as a substance, a collection of things, events, or ideas, or the contents of something in a general way without mentioning the thing itself by name.

hall [hɔ:l] n. 현관; 복도; 넓은 방
The hall in a house or flat is the area just inside the front door, into which some of the other rooms open.

float [flout] v. (물 위나 공중에서) 떠가다; (물에) 뜨다; n. 부표
Something that floats in or through the air hangs in it or moves slowly and gently through it.

hallway [hɔ́:lwèi] n. 복도; 통로; 현관
A hallway in a building is a long passage with doors into rooms on both sides of it.

realize [ríːəlàiz] v. 깨닫다, 알아차리다; 실현하다, 달성하다
If you realize that something is true, you become aware of that fact or understand it.

be supposed to idiom ~해야 한다, ~하기로 되어 있다
If you say that something is supposed to happen, you mean that it is planned or expected.

slurp [sləːrp] v. 후루룩 마시다; 후루룩 하는 소리를 내다; n. 훌쩍훌쩍 마시는 소리
If you slurp a liquid, you drink it noisily.

* **alphabetical** [ælfəbétikəl] a. 알파벳순의
Alphabetical means arranged according to the normal order of the letters in the alphabet.

order [ɔ́:rdər] n. 순서; 주문; 명령; v. 명령을 내리다; 주문하다
If a set of things are arranged or done in a particular order, they are arranged or done so one thing follows another, often according to a particular factor such as importance.

banish [bǽniʃ] v. 제거하다; 사라지게 하다; 추방하다
If you banish something unpleasant, you get rid of it.

ritual [rítʃuəl] n. (종교적인) 의례; 의식과 같은 일
A ritual is a religious service or other ceremony which involves a series of actions performed in a fixed order.

evil [íːvəl] a. 사악한, 악랄한; 유해한; 악마의; n. 악
If you describe someone as evil, you mean that they are very wicked by nature and take pleasure in doing things that harm other people.

复습spirit [spírit] n. 유령, 정령; 영혼; 기분, 마음; 태도
A spirit is a ghost or supernatural being.

복습demon [díːmən] n. 악령, 악마
A demon is an evil spirit.

복습dwell [dwel] v. 살다, 거주하다
If you dwell somewhere, you live there.

복습filth [filθ] n. 오물, 쓰레기
Filth is a disgusting amount of dirt.

all at once idiom 갑자기
If something happens all at once, it happens suddenly, often when you are not expecting it to happen.

*drawer [drɔːr] n. 서랍
A drawer is part of a desk, chest, or other piece of furniture that is shaped like a box and is designed for putting things in.

*handwriting [hǽndraitiŋ] n. (손으로 쓴) 글씨체, 필체
Your handwriting is your style of writing with a pen or pencil.

*kindly [káindli] ad. 제발, 부디; 친절하게, 다정하게
If someone asks you to kindly do something, they are asking you in a way which shows that they have authority over you, or that they are angry with you.

*insult [insʌ́lt] v. 모욕하다; n. 모욕(적인 말·행동)
If someone insults you, they say or do something that is rude or offensive.

복습certain [səːrtn] a. 확실한, 틀림없는 (certainly ad. 틀림없이, 분명히)
If you are certain about something, you firmly believe it is true and have no doubt about it.

복습stare [stɛər] v. 빤히 쳐다보다, 응시하다; n. 빤히 쳐다보기, 응시
If you stare at someone or something, you look at them for a long time.

scribble [skríbl] v. 갈겨쓰다, 휘갈기다; 낙서하다; n. 낙서
If you scribble something, you write it quickly and roughly.

pop [pap] v. 눈이 휘둥그레지다; 펑 터지다, 터뜨리다; n. 펑 (하는 소리)
If your eyes pop, you look very surprised or excited when you see something.

trick [trik] n. 솜씨, 재주; 속임수; 요령; v. 속이다, 속임수를 쓰다
A trick is a clever or skillful action that someone does in order to entertain people.

address [ədrés] v. 호칭으로 부르다; 말을 걸다; 연설하다; 주소를 쓰다; n. 주소; 연설
If you address someone by a name or a title, you call them that name or title when you talk or write to them.

pleased [pli:zd] a. 기쁜, 기뻐하는
If you are pleased, you are happy about something or satisfied with something.

acquaintance [əkwéintəns] n. 아는 사람, 지인
(make one's acquaintance idiom ~을 처음으로 만나다)
When you make someone's acquaintance, you meet them for the first time and get to know them a little.

sense [sens] v. 감지하다, 느끼다; (기계가) 탐지하다; n. 감각; 지각, 일리; 느낌
If you sense something, you become aware of it or you realize it, although it is not very obvious.

present [preznt] ① a. 있는; 현재의; n. 현재 (presence n. 있음, 존재(함))
② v. 보여 주다; 주다, 수여하다
Someone's presence in a place is the fact that they are there.

cupboard [kʌ́bərd] n. 식기장, 찬장
A cupboard is a piece of furniture that has one or two doors, usually contains shelves, and is used to store things.

content [kántent] ① n. (pl.) 내용물; 내용 ② a. 만족하는; v. 만족시키다
The contents of a container such as a bottle, box, or room are the things that are inside it.

Chapter 8

1. **How did Wanda and Cecil feel about each other?**

   A. They had a bad impression of each other.

   B. They felt thankful to have met each other.

   C. Wanda was more fond of Cecil than he was of her.

   D. Cecil was more willing to be friends than Wanda was.

2. **Why did Zack yell at Wanda and Cecil?**

   A. Their voices got too loud.

   B. Their behavior was unacceptable.

   C. They were treating everyone like babies.

   D. They made Vernon get injured.

3. Why did Wanda and Cecil need to get along?

   A. They belonged to the same family.
   B. They could not leave the neighborhood alone.
   C. They did not have other spirits to play with.
   D. They were going to live with Zack for a long time.

4. Why did Zack suggest the Adventureland Amusement Park?

   A. Wanda and Cecil could be useful there.
   B. Wanda and Cecil could meet other spirits there.
   C. Wanda and Cecil could live a quiet life there.
   D. Wanda and Cecil could build their own house there.

5. What happened after Wanda and Cecil went to Adventureland?

   A. People found out about them and they became famous.
   B. Zack was happy that he never had to see them again.
   C. The haunted house became too spooky and closed down.
   D. Zack occasionally heard about the haunted house on the news.

Check Your Reading Speed
1분에 몇 단어를 읽는지 리딩 속도를 측정해보세요.

$$\frac{774 \text{ words}}{\text{reading time ( ) sec}} \times 60 = (\quad) \text{ wPM}$$

Build Your Vocabulary

scribble [skribl] v. 갈겨쓰다, 휘갈기다; 낙서하다; n. 낙서
If you scribble something, you write it quickly and roughly.

arrange [əréindʒ] v. 배열하다, 정리하다; 마련하다, 처리하다 (rearrange v. 재배열하다)
If you rearrange things, you change the way in which they are organized or ordered.

hit it off idiom (만나자마자) 서로 잘 맞다, 서로 잘 통하다
If two people hit it off, they like each other and become friendly as soon as they meet.

skid [skid] v. 미끄러지다; n. (차량의) 미끄러짐
If a vehicle skids, it slides sideways or forward while moving, for example when you are trying to stop it suddenly on a wet road.

spell [spel] v. (문자들이 어떤 단어를) 만들다; 철자를 맞게 쓰다; n. 주문; 마법
When you spell out a word, you write or speak each letter in the word in the correct order.

★ **crude** [kruːd] a. 막된, 상스러운; 대충의, 대강의; 원래 그대로의
If you describe someone as crude, you disapprove of them because they speak or behave in a rude, offensive, or unsophisticated way.

uneducated [ʌnédʒukèitid] a. 교육을 못 받은; 무지한
Someone who is uneducated has not received much education.

★ unacceptable [ʌnəkséptəbl] a. 받아들일 수 없는
(unacceptably ad. 받아들이기 힘든 정도로)
If you describe something as unacceptable, you strongly disapprove of it or object to it and feel that it should not be allowed to continue.

복습 messy [mési] a. 지저분한, 엉망인; 골치 아픈
Something that is messy is dirty or untidy.

snob [snab] n. (잘난 척하는) 속물, 고상한 척하는 사람
If you call someone a snob, you disapprove of them because they behave as if they are superior to other people because of their intelligence or taste.

‡ common [kámən] a. 공통의, 공동의; 흔한; 평범한; n. 공유지, 공원
(have in common idiom 공통점이 있다)
If two or more things have something in common, they have the same characteristic or feature.

복습 and all idiom ~을 포함하여
You use and all when you want to emphasize that what you are talking about includes the thing mentioned, especially when this is surprising or unusual.

get along idiom 사이좋게 지내다; 어울리다
If people get along, they like each other and are friendly to each other.

복습 sweat [swet] v. 땀을 흘리다; 식은땀을 흘리다, 불안해하다; n. 땀; 노력, 수고
When you sweat, you produce liquid on the surface of your skin when you are hot, nervous, or ill.

take back idiom (말을) 취소하다
If you take something back, you admit that something that you said or thought is wrong.

복습 yank [jæŋk] v. 확 잡아당기다; n. 홱 잡아당기기
If you yank someone or something somewhere, you pull them there suddenly and with a lot of force.

CHAPTER 8

underpants [ʌ́ndərpænts] n. (남성용·여성용) 팬티
Underpants are a piece of underwear which have two holes to put your legs through and elastic around the top to hold them up round your waist or hips.

dinosaur [dáinəsɔ̀ːr] n. 공룡
Dinosaurs were large reptiles which lived in prehistoric times.

bend [bend] v. (bent-bent) (몸·머리를) 굽히다, 숙이다; 구부리다; n. (도로·강의) 굽이
When you bend, you move the top part of your body downward and forward.

reach [riːtʃ] v. (손이) 닿다; ~에 이르다; (손·팔을) 뻗다; n. (닿을 수 있는) 거리
If you can reach something, you are able to touch it by stretching out your arm or leg.

violent [váiələnt] a. 폭력적인, 난폭한; 지독한; 격렬한 (violently ad. 난폭하게, 거칠게)
If you do something violently, you do it with a lot of force in a way that is very difficult to control.

tuck [tʌk] v. (옷·시트의 자락을) 집어넣다; 끼워 넣다; n. 주름, 단
If you tuck something somewhere, you put it there so that it is safe, comfortable, or neat.

unseen [ʌnsíːn] a. 눈에 보이지 않는; 처음 보는
You can use unseen to describe things which people cannot see.

cut out idiom 그만두다; ~을 삭제하다
If you tell someone to cut something out, you are telling them in an irritated way to stop it.

instant [instənt] n. (바로 그) 순간; 아주 짧은 동안; a. 즉각적인
If you say that something happens at a particular instant, you mean that it happens at exactly the time you have been referring to, and you are usually suggesting that it happens quickly or immediately.

yell [jel] v. 고함치다, 소리 지르다; n. 고함, 외침
If you yell, you shout loudly, usually because you are excited, angry, or in pain.

tolerate [tálərèit] v. 용인하다; (불쾌한 일을) 참다; 견디다
If you tolerate a situation or person, you accept them although you do not particularly like them.

hurt [həːrt] a. 기분이 상한, (마음에) 상처를 입은; 다친; v. 다치게 하다; 아프다
If you are hurt, you are upset because of something that someone has said or done.

neighbor [néibər] n. 이웃; 동료; 동포 (neighborhood n. 인근, 근처)
The neighborhood of a place or person is the area or the people around them.

no way idiom 절대로 안 돼; 말도 안 돼; 싫어
You can say no way as an emphatic way of saying no.

reside [rizáid] v. 살다, 거주하다; 존재하다
If someone resides somewhere, they live there or are staying there.

gang [gæŋ] n. 친구들, 무리; 범죄 조직
The gang is a group of friends who frequently meet.

amusement park [əmjúːzmənt paːrk] n. 놀이공원
An amusement park is a place where people pay to ride on various machines for entertainment or try to win prizes in games.

haunt [hɔːnt] v. (어떤 장소에) 귀신이 나타나다; (불쾌한 생각이) 계속 떠오르다
(haunted house n. (놀이공원의) 유령의 집; 흉가)
A haunted house in an amusement park is a house decorated to be spooky that serves as an attraction, usually around Halloween.

pathetic [pəθétik] a. 한심한; 불쌍한, 애처로운
If you describe someone or something as pathetic, you mean that they make you feel impatient or angry, often because they are weak or not very good.

scare [skɛər] v. 놀라게 하다; 무서워하다; n. 불안(감); 놀람, 공포
If something scares you, it frightens or worries you.

pro [prou] n. (= professional) 전문가, 프로; a. 전문적인, 직업 선수의
A pro is a professional who has a lot of experience with a particular type of situation.

whip into shape idiom ~을 정상화하다, ~가 모양을 갖추게 하다
If you whip someone or something into shape, you use whatever methods are necessary to change or improve them so that they are in the condition that you want them to be in.

in no time idiom 당장에, 곧
If something happens in no time, it happens almost immediately or very quickly.

bet [bet] v. (~이) 틀림없다; 내기하다; n. 짐작, 추측; 내기
You use expressions such as 'I bet,' 'I'll bet,' and 'you can bet' to indicate that you are sure something is true.

scare the daylights out of idiom ~에게 잔뜩 겁을 주다
If someone or something scares the daylights out of you, they make you feel extremely anxious or afraid.

willing [wíliŋ] a. 기꺼이 ~하는; 자발적인
If someone is willing to do something, they are fairly happy about doing it and will do it if they are asked or required to do it.

take over idiom 장악하다, 탈취하다; (~을) 인계받다
If you take over something, you take control of it.

intrigue [intríːg] v. 강한 흥미를 불러일으키다; 음모를 꾸미다; n. 음모; 흥미로움
(intriguing a. 아주 흥미로운)
If you describe something as intriguing, you mean that it is interesting or strange.

challenge [tʃǽlindʒ] n. 도전; 저항; v. 도전하다; 도전 의식을 북돋우다
A challenge is something new and difficult which requires great effort and determination.

★ **relieve** [rilíːv] v. 안도하게 하다; (불쾌감·고통 등을) 없애 주다; 완화하다 (relieved a. 안도한)
If you are relieved, you feel happy because something unpleasant has not happened or is no longer happening.

복습 **run** [rʌn] v. 운영하다; 달리다; (필름 등을) 돌리다, 재생시키다; n. 달리기; 연속
If you run something such as a business or an activity, you are in charge of it or you organize it.

dream up idiom (말도 안 되는 내용을) 생각해 내다
If you dream up a new idea or plan, you think of it, especially one that is silly or unusual.

복습 **spooky** [spúːki] a. 으스스한, 귀신이 나올 것 같은
If you say that something is spooky, you mean that it is strange or frightening in a way that makes you think of ghosts.

복습 **trick** [trik] n. 속임수; 요령; 솜씨, 재주; v. 속이다, 속임수를 쓰다
A trick is an action that is intended to deceive someone.

‡ **celebrate** [sélədrèit] v. 기념하다, 축하하다
If you celebrate, you do something enjoyable because of a special occasion or to mark someone's success.

번역

1장

그 으스스한 일이 처음으로 일어났을 때, 저는 그것이 으스스하다는 것을 깨닫지도 못했습니다. 이유는 몰라도, 제가 으스스한 것들을 좋아하기 때문일 거예요... 제 말은 그것들이 정말로 무섭지 않다면요, 이 경우에는 그렇게 많이 무섭지는 않았던 것 같아요.

아, 제가 누구인지 말해야겠군요. 제 이름은 잭(Zack)입니다. 열 살이고요. 그리고 제 생각에 저는 항상 기이한 것에 관심을 좀 가져온 것 같습니다. 늑대인간(werewolf)과 뱀파이어(vampire)와 좀비(zombie) 그리고 욕실 안으로 들어가서 수도꼭지를 틀면 피가 쏟아져 나오는 집 같은 것들. 그런 것에 말이에요.

솔직히 말하자면, 저는 제가 방금 말한 것들 중 어떤 것도 본 적이 없습니다. 하긴 저는 겨우 열 살인걸요.

어쨌든, 다시 제 이야기를 할게요. 몇 달 전 어느 밤, 저는 갑자기 잠에서 깼습니다. 우리 아파트에 있는 모든 문들이 계속해서 열렸다가 닫혔습니다. 아빠 방으로 가는 문, 제 침실 문, 제 욕실 문, 제 벽장으로 가는 문까지. 그냥 저절로 열렸다가 닫혔습니다. 저는 생각했습니다, 에이, 별 거 아냐. 바람이나 뭐 그런 거겠지. 그래서 저는 다시 잠이 들었습니다. 그게 실제로 무엇이었는지 알

았다면, 저는 아마 그렇게 태연하지 못했을 거예요.

다음 날 아침에 잠에서 깼을 때, 제가 처음으로 알아차린 것은 제 방이 엉망이라는 것이었습니다. 자 저는 여러분들이 오해하지 않기를 바랍니다. 제 방은 언제나 꽤 지저분해요. 하지만 오늘 아침은, 평소보다 훨씬 더 엉망이었습니다.

전날 밤에 제가 벗어서 바닥에 던져 놓았던 바지가 지금은 창문 블라인드 롤러에 걸려 있었습니다. 제가 방구석에 아무렇게나 던져 버렸던 신발은 쓰레기통 안에 들어 있었습니다. 제 티셔츠는 천장의 전등에 걸려 있었습니다. 제 팬티는 곰 인형의 머리 위에 씌워져 있었습니다. 이 일들 중 어떤 것도 하지 않았다고 저는 꽤나 확신했습니다. 게다가 누가 그랬는지 알지도 못했습니다.

저는 할 수 있는 한 빨리 그것들을 치웠습니다. 딱히 제가 제 방을 치우는 것을 좋아해서 그런 것은 아니에요. 아빠가 제 방에 들어와서, "이게 다 뭐니?"라고 말하는 것을 원하지 않았을 뿐입니다. 우리 아빠는 멋지고, 저는 그를 정말 좋아합니다. 그런데 아빠는 좀 깔끔쟁이입니다. 그리고 저는 그가 제 방으로 들어와서, "이게 다 뭐니?"라고 말하는 것을 정말 참을 수 없습니다.

방을 다 치우자마자, 저는 양치를 하러 갔습니다. 그리고 바로 그곳에서 저

는 더 많은 우스꽝스러운 일들을 보게 되었습니다. 누군가가 제 욕실 거울 전체에 비누를 문질러 놓았습니다. 그리고 변기 시트 아래에는 비닐 랩(Saran Wrap)을 깔아 놓았습니다. 저에게 장난을 치려고 어떤 아이가 숨어 들어왔던 것일까요? 아니면 뭔가 기괴한 일이 여기서 일어나고 있는 걸까요?

"잭, 너 일어났니?" 아빠가 복도에서 외쳤습니다.

"네, 아빠." 저는 소리쳐 대답했습니다.

그는 제 침실 문 안으로 자신의 머리를 집어넣었습니다.

"오-이런." 그가 말했습니다.

저는 제 침실로 돌아갔고, 제 입이 떡 벌어졌습니다. 제 방이 다시 엉망이 되어 있었습니다. 게다가, 모든 전선이 나비 모양 매듭으로 묶여 있었습니다. 액자에 넣어진 저의 레아 할머니(Grandma Leah)의 사진 위에는 콧수염과 턱수염이 그려져 있었습니다. 이것은 아이가 장난치는 게 아니었습니다. 뭔가 기이한 일이 일어나고 있었습니다!

"이게 다 뭐니?" 아빠가 말했습니다.

방이 엉망인 것에 아빠가 정말 화가 났다는 것을 저는 알 수 있었습니다. 엄마와 아빠는 몇 년 전 이혼했습니다. 이제 저는 일부 시간은 아빠와 보내고, 일부 시간은 엄마와 보내고 있습니다. 아빠의 집은 엄마의 집보다 언제나 더 깨끗했습니다. 정확하게는, 여태까지는 말이에요.

"아빠." 제가 말했습니다. "저 방금 제 방을 청소했어요. 네? 양치하러 욕실로 들어가기 바로 전까지요. 맹세해요. 저도 이게 이상하게 들린다는 걸 알아요. 하지만 저는 우리 집에 귀신이 있거나 뭐 그런 것 같아요."

"잭, 난 네가 가끔 조심성이 없거나 네 방을 지저분하게 둔다고 해도 신경 쓰지 않는단다." 아빠는 말했습니다. "그렇지만 정말로 네가 거짓말을 하지는 말았으면 좋겠구나."

"거짓말을 하고 있는 게 아니에요." 제가 말했습니다. "저 진짜로 방금 전에 방 청소를 다 했어요. 저는 제 방을 이런 상태로 두지 않았어요."

아빠의 얼굴에 떠오른 표정으로 보아 그가 여전히 제 말을 믿지 않는다는 것을 저는 알 수 있었습니다. 그런데 바로 그 순간, 제 책장 꼭대기 위에 있는 TV가 공중으로 부드럽게 떠올랐습니다. 그러고 나서 그것은 천천히 그리고 소리 없이 방을 가로질러 날아가서 제 서랍장 위에 내려앉았습니다.

아빠는 그것이 이동하는 것을 보았습니다. 그의 두 눈이 정말 커졌습니다. 제 눈도 마찬가지였습니다.

"있잖아, 잭." 한참 있다가 아빠가 말했습니다. "결국 네 말을 믿어야 할 것

번역

같구나."

2장

아빠와 저는 제 방에서 달려 나와서 부엌으로 도망쳤습니다. 우리는 발판 사다리로 문을 막았습니다. 그러고 나서 우리는 돌아섰습니다.

이크! 여기는 훨씬 더 심했습니다!

식탁에는 이미 아침 식사가 차려져 있었습니다. 단지, 식탁이 뒤집힌 상태에서 차려져 있었지요.

찬장은 문이 열려 있었고 텅 비어 있었습니다. 모든 접시들은 한 줄로 매우 높이 쌓여 있었는데, 그것들은 앞뒤로 불안하게 흔들리고 있었습니다.

더 이상 의심할 여지가 없었습니다. 우리 집에 폴터가이스트(poltergeist)가 있었습니다. 저는 이것에 대해 책을 읽어 본 적이 있어서, 알고 있습니다. 여러분이 모를까 봐 말하자면, 폴터가이스트는 유령 같은 것입니다. 문제를 일으키기 좋아하는 유령이요. 그 유령들은 적어도 한 명의 아이가 있는 집에 주로 나타나고, 그들은 집을 엉망으로 만들어 버리지요.

저는 아빠가 이 모든 상황을 어떻게 받아들이는지 보려고 아빠를 쳐다보았습니다.

"오늘 밤에 우리가 라마다 인(Ramada Inn)에서 묵으면 어떨까?" 아빠가 물었습니다.

"아, 저는 그런 낯선 모텔 방에서 밤을 보내고 싶지 않아요." 제가 말했습니다.

플랩잭(Flapjack)이 가스레인지 위에서 구워지기 시작했습니다. 그것들은 저절로 공중으로 튕겨 올라갔습니다. 그러더니 그것들은 뒤집어졌고 팬 위에 다시 내려앉았습니다.

매우 높게 쌓인 접시 무더기가 한 방향으로, 그리고 반대 방향으로 불안정하게 흔들렸습니다. 그러더니 몹시 크고 요란한 소리를 내며 무너졌습니다. 깨진 접시 조각들은 사방으로 날아갔습니다.

냉장고 문이 확 열렸고, 그 안에 있던 모든 음식들이 바닥으로 쏟아져 나왔습니다.

"다른 한편으로는." 제가 말했습니다. "라마다 인이 정말 괜찮을 수 있다고 들었어요."

3장

학교에서 공부하는 것이 저에게 정말 힘들었습니다. 그리고 뉴욕시에 있는 호러스 하이드-화이트 남학교(Horace Hyde-White School for Boys)에서는, 할 일이 정말 많습니다.

저는 유령에 대해 계속 생각하고 있었습니다. 우리 아빠의 아파트에서 지금 무슨 일이 일어나고 있는지 누가 알 수 있겠어요? 저는 유령에 대해 너무 골똘히 생각하고 있던 나머지 수업 시간에 우리가 무엇을 하고 있는지에 대해 완전히 무시하고 있었던 게 분명합니다.

어느 순간 저의 영어 선생님, 호프만 선생님(Mr. Hoffman)이, 저에게 뭔가를 질문했습니다. 저는 깜짝 놀라서, 고개를 들었습니다.

"그래서, 잭." 호프만 선생님이 말했습니다. "네 의견은 뭐니?"

"제 의견이요?" 제가 말했습니다. 저는 목을 가다듬었고 긴장을 풀려고 애썼습니다.

"그래."

"어, 그게." 저는 시간을 끌면서, 말했습니다. "선생님, 아시다시피, 그 질문을 살펴보는 방식은 아주 많아요. 저는 너무 급하게 의견을 정하고 싶지 않습니다."

"잭." 선생님은 말했습니다. "내 생각에는 네가 우리의 토론을 듣고 있지 않았던 것 같구나."

"어, 아니요, 제가 그러지 않았던 것 같습니다, 선생님." 저는 말했습니다. "정말 죄송해요. 그렇지만 전 오늘 마음이 복잡해요."

"좋아, 그렇게 솔직하게 말해 줘서 고맙구나." 선생님이 말했습니다. "오늘 네가 학교 공부보다 더 중요하게 생각하고 있는 것은 뭐니?"

"폴터가이스트요."

학생들 몇 명이 웃기 시작했습니다.

"폴터가이스트라고?"

"네, 선생님." 저는 말했습니다. "혹시 그것들에 관해서 아시는 것이 있나요?"

"글쎄다." 호프만 선생님이 말했습니다. "나는 그 말이 독일어로 '시끄러운 유령'을 의미한다는 것은 알고 있단다. 그런데 무슨 일 때문에 너는 폴터가이스트에 대해 생각하고 있는 거니?"

"음." 저는 말했습니다. "이 말이 정말 믿기 어렵다는 것을 저도 알아요. 하지만 어떤 보이지 않는 힘이 우리 아빠의 아파트를 망가뜨리고 있어요. 그리고 저는 그게 유령일지도 모른다고 생각했어요. . . 폴터가이스트요."

교실의 아이들이 너무 심하게 웃어서 그들은 하마터면 의자에서 떨어질 뻔했습니다. 어떤 아이들은 "아, 맞아, 잭." 또는, "그럼, 물론이지, 잭."이라고 말했습니다.

"누구든 유령을 믿는 사람은 말이야." 버논 만토이펠(Vernon Manteuffel)이라는 이름의 아이가 말했습니다. "미신을 믿는 바보 멍청이야."

더 많은 웃음소리가 나왔습니다.

"닥쳐, 버논." 제가 말했습니다. 버논

만토이펠은 땀을 많이 흘리고 주말에만 목욕을 합니다. 그는 자기가 씹던 풍선껌을 자신의 귀 뒤에 붙여 놓습니다. 그는 3학년 이후로 체육복을 한 번도 세탁하지 않았다고 떠벌립니다. 그는 어떤 면에서는 학교의 전설 같은 사람입니다.

"자, 애들아, 그만하면 되었다." 호프만 선생님이 말했습니다.

"넌 또한, 어쩌면 이의 요정(Tooth Fairy)이 있다는 것도 믿겠네." 버논 만토이펠이 말했습니다.

"닥치라고, 버논." 제가 말했습니다. 저는 닥치라는 말보다 뭔가 더 멋진 말을 생각해 낼 수 있었기를 바랐습니다. 하지만 저는 그러지 못했습니다.

"내가 입 닥치게 해 봐, 멍청아." 버논이 말했습니다.

"잭! 버논!" 호프만 선생님이 소리쳤습니다. "나는 싸우는 것을 용납하지 않는단다. 너희 둘 중 한 명이라도 한 마디만 더 하면 둘 다 방과 후에 남게 될 거야."

버논과 저는 둘 다 아주 조용해졌습니다.

"훨씬 낫구나." 호프만 선생님이 말했습니다. "있잖니, 나는 초자연적인 것을 믿지 않지만, 그걸 믿는 사람들이 정말 많단다. 그리고 그들이 다 미신을 믿는 바보 멍청이는 아니야, 버논. 추천하자면, 잭, 너는 도서관에 가서 조사를 좀 해 보는 것이 좋겠구나."

그것은 모든 문제에 대한 호프만 선생님의 해결 방법이었습니다. 도서관에 가는 것 말입니다. 그런데, 생각해 보니까, 그것은 나쁜 생각은 아니었습니다.

4장

학교가 끝난 후 저는 공공 도서관으로 바로 달려갔습니다. 저는 백과사전에서 유령과 폴터가이스트를 찾아 보았습니다. 백과사전에는 재미있는 내용들이 나와 있었습니다. 그렇지만 그것들을 없애는 방법에 대해서는 나와 있지 않았습니다. 그래서 저는 도움을 청하기 위해 사서에게 갔습니다.

사서, 반 담 선생님(Mr. Van Damm)은, 숱이 많은 콧수염을 기르고 있으며, 몹시 힘이 센 두 팔을 지녔습니다. 그 이유는 그가 역기 운동하는 것을 정말 좋아하기 때문입니다. 그는 덩치가 크고, 힘이 센 남자이지만, 그는 참고 도서에 대해서도 정말 잘 알고 있습니다.

"실례합니다, 선생님." 제가 말했습니다. "유령을 쫓아내는 방법 같은 것은 정확히 어디에서 찾을 수 있을까요?"

반 담 선생님은 저를 보고 인상을 썼습니다. 제가 선생님을 놀리고 있다고 생각하지 않기를 저는 바랐습니다. 그는 놀림을 받는 것을 좋아하는 사람은 아닌 것 같았습니다.

"진심이니?" 그는 물었습니다.

"이보다 더 진지할 수는 없어요, 선생님." 제가 말했습니다. "어떤 사람들 집에 바퀴벌레가 있듯이 저희 집에는 유령이 있어요."

"그렇다면 네가 원하는 것은 퇴치 의식이겠구나." 그는 말했습니다. "퇴치 의식은 영적인 세계에서는 바퀴벌레 퇴치약 같은 거야. 저쪽 계단 아래에 있는 흑마술 부분에서 찾을 수 있단다."

저는 사서 선생님에게 감사 인사를 했고 계단 아래에서 흑마술에 대한 책을 찾으러 갔습니다. 여러분이 잘 모를까 봐 설명하자면, 정장용 모자에서 토끼를 꺼내는 것은 선의의 마술이라고 부릅니다. 사람들에게 저주를 걸거나 사악한 영혼들을 가지고 장난을 치는 것은 흑마술이라고 합니다.

저는 폴터가이스트에 대한 것을 모두 읽었습니다. 흑마술에 대한 어떤 책에서, 저는 마침내 퇴치 의식을 찾아냈습니다. 검정색 양초 일곱 개에 불을 붙이고 이 말을 일곱 번 말해야 합니다:

"오, 사악한 유령이여, 오, 더러운 곳에 거주하며, 어둡고, 냄새 나는 곳에 살고 있는 위대하고 끔찍한 악령이여, 이제 내 말을 들어라: 나는 너를 쫓아내겠다! 나는 너에게 떠날 것을 명령한다! 나는 너에게 이곳을 떠나라고 명령하노라! 오, 어둠 속에 오는 영혼이여, 오, 가장 사나운 밤의 악령이여, 코가 뒤집어지고, 얼굴은 위아래가 바뀌었으며, 옷은 안팎이 뒤집어져서 속옷이 보이는 악령이여, 일어나 이곳에서 당장 사라져라!"

저에게 들리기로는 이 악령들은 모두 고대 영국이나 뭐 그런 곳에서 죽은 사람들 같았습니다. 그리고 아마도 그것이 그들이 알아들을 수 있는 유일한 언어인가 봅니다. 죽은 미국 사람들에게는 그렇게 말할 필요가 없다고 저는 생각합니다. 아니면, 아마도 우리 아빠의 아파트를 엉망으로 만들고 있는 그 유령은 고대 영국에서 온 죽은 노인이었을 지도 모릅니다. 그렇다면, 그 유령은 우리가 하는 말을 알아들을 것입니다.

저는 제 책을 들고 도서 대출대로 갔습니다. 저는 역시 유령과 악령에 대한 책을 잔뜩 가지고 있는 어떤 덩치 큰 아이 뒤에 줄을 섰습니다. 그 아이는 땀을 무척 많이 흘리고 있었습니다.

"버논!" 제가 말했습니다. "너 그 책들을 가지고 뭐 하고 있니? 유령을 믿는 사람은 누구나 미신을 믿는 바보 멍청이라고 네가 말했잖아."

그 말을 한 사람이 저라는 것을 보자 버논의 두 눈이 휘둥그레졌습니다. 그의 얼굴이 너무 시뻘게져서, 저는 그의

번역

혈관이 터질지도 모른다고 생각했습니다. "나는 그런 거 아–안 믿어." 그는 더 듬거리며 말했습니다.

그의 말은 그다지 설득력 있게 들리지 않았습니다.

"그러면 너는 왜 유령에 대한 책을 빌리고 있어?"

"내가 너에게 말해 주면, 그걸 비밀로 하겠다고 약속할 거야?"

"어쩌면."

"실은 말야." 불안한 듯 주위를 살피고 속삭이는 소리로 목소리를 낮추면서, 버논이 말했습니다. "우리 아파트에서도 기괴한 일이 벌어지고 있어."

"네 말은 보이지 않는 힘이 네 집을 엉망으로 만들고 있다는 거야?" 놀라서, 저는 물었습니다.

"아니, 그거보다 더 좋지 않아, 잭." 그가 말했습니다. "훨씬 더 심해. 보이지 않는 힘이 집을 깨끗하게 정리하고 있어."

"나에게는 그렇게 나쁘게 들리지 않아." 우리 아빠의 아파트에서 무슨 일들이 일어나고 있는지를 기억하면서, 제가 말했습니다.

"너는 이해 못 해." 그가 말했습니다. "내 방의 물건들이 보이지 않게 다시 정리되어 있어. 내가 원하는 방식이 아니라, 다른 누군가가 원하는 방식으로 말이야. 내가 침대에서 나와; 그러면 침대가 스스로 정리를 해. 시트와 담요가 저절로 아주 팽팽하게 집어넣어져서 그 위에서 25센트 동전을 튕길 수도 있어. 어떤 때는 그런 일이 내가 아직 침대에 누워 있을 때도 일어나. 잭, 네 생각에 우리 집에도 폴터가이스트가 있는 것 같니?"

"만약 그렇다면." 빌린 책을 가지고 문 쪽으로 가면서, 저는 말했습니다. "우리 집에 있는 것보다 훨씬 더 기괴하네."

"있지, 잭!" 그는 말했습니다. "나 좀 도와줄 수 없을까?"

"나중에 연락할게." 저는 말했습니다.

저는 도서관 계단에 버논을 두고 떠났습니다. 퇴치 의식이 저에게 통한다면, 아마도 제가 그것을 하는 방법을 버논에게도 알려 줄 수 있겠지요. 제가 전에도 말했지만, 그는 제가 좋아하는 아이는 아닙니다. 하지만 저는 그저 그 아이가 조금 안됐다고 생각했습니다 — 제 말은, 그런 깔끔함과 함께 살아야 한다는 것이 말입니다.

저는 길모퉁이에 있는 파티용품 가게에 들렀습니다. 저는 검정색 양초 일곱 개를 샀습니다. 그런 뒤 저는 퇴치 의식을 하기 위해 아빠의 아파트로 향했습니다. 저는 죽은 사람들, 특히 악령들에게 그다지 말을 걸고 싶지는 않습니다. 하지만 저는 그것이 우리의 유일한 희망이라고 생각했습니다.

5장

흑마술에 대한 제 책과 검정색 양초 일곱 개를 들고 제가 집으로 돌아왔을 때, 아빠는 기겁하고 있었습니다.

처음에는 제가 집에 늦게 와서 아빠가 저에게 화가 많이 난 거라고 생각했습니다. 그러나 그때 저는 전혀 그것 때문이 아니라는 걸 알았습니다. 아파트 안의 상황이 훨씬 더 나빠졌습니다. 그곳은 완전히 엉망이 되어 있었을 뿐만 아니라, 집안의 모든 물건 위에 투명하고 끈적거리는 물질이 있었습니다. 그것은 마치 메이플 시럽(maple syrup)과 고무 접착제(rubber cement)의 혼합물 같았습니다.

"이게 뭐니?" 아빠가 꺽꺽거리듯 말했습니다. 그는 너무 당황한 나머지 거의 말을 할 수 없었습니다.

"저는 도서관에서 방금 이것에 대해 읽었어요." 제가 말했습니다. "이건 엑토플라즘(ectoplasm)이라는 거예요. 그건 주변에 유령들이 있을 때 생기는 물질이에요."

저는 아빠와 아빠의 멋진 아파트에 일어난 일 때문에 마음이 좋지 않았습니다. 아빠의 눈은 약간 멍했습니다. 아빠는 전쟁 영화에 나오는 사람처럼 보였습니다. 어쩔 줄 모르는 상태였어요.

그의 다리는 후들거렸습니다.

저는 제가 나서야 한다는 것을 알았습니다. 저는 흑마술에 관한 책을 아빠에게 보여 주었고 퇴치 의식을 할 거라고 말했습니다. 그는 앞을 똑바로 바라보면서, 고개를 끄덕였습니다.

그런 뒤 우리는 검은 양초 일곱 개에 불을 붙였습니다. 그리고 저는 제가 느끼는 것보다 더 자신감 있게 들리기를 바라며 큰 소리로 읽기 시작했습니다: "오, 사악한 유령이여, 오, 더러운 곳에 거주하며, 어둡고, 냄새 나는 곳에 살고 있는 위대하고 끔찍한 악령이여, 이제 내 말을 들어라. . . ."

저는 계속 읽었습니다. 그러나 아무 일도 일어나지 않았습니다. 아무 일도요. 그래서 저는 읽기를 멈추었고, 책을 탁 내려놓았고, 아빠를 바라보았습니다.

"죄송해요." 제가 말했습니다. "이건 효과가 없네요."

그 순간 우리는 아주 커다란 소리를 들었습니다. 선반 위에 있던 커다란 땅콩 M&M 초콜릿 봉지가 터졌습니다. M&M 초콜릿들이 모두 위로 날아갔습니다. 그것들은 천장에 부딪친 뒤, 그곳에 붙었습니다. 천장에 붙은 것은 조합되어 메시지가 되었습니다. 그것은 이렇게 쓰여 있었습니다:

그래 그래, 나 여기 있어 이제 뭐?

번역

(OK OK, HERE I AM WHAT NOW?)

"오, 세상에." 저는 조용히 말했습니다.

"오, 세상에나." 아빠가 말했습니다.

저는 이 일을 믿을 수가 없었습니다. 제가 실제로 악령과 접촉한 것입니다. 죽은 사람의 실제 영혼과 말입니다.

솔직히 말하자면, 저는 정말 겁이 났습니다. 저는 마치 프로즌 요구르트를 꺼내려고 냉동실 문을 막 열었고, 모든 냉기가 제 위로 떨어졌을 때처럼, 끔찍하게 오싹한 기분이 들었습니다. 제 머리와 등과 목의 피부가 따끔거리기 시작했습니다.

"우리 이제 무엇을 해야 하죠?" 저는 속삭였습니다.

"나도 모르겠다." 아빠가 말했습니다. 그의 목소리는 여전히 좀 떨리고 있었습니다. 그렇지만 그는 좀 덜 멍해 보였습니다. "그것에게 뭔가 물어보는 게 어떨까?" 아빠가 말했습니다.

"오, 이곳에 살고 계신 유령이여." 저는 낮고, 공손한 어조로 말했습니다. "당신이 우리 아파트를 엉망으로 만들었던 유령과 같은 유령인가요?"

부드럽고, 긁히는 소리가 나면서 천장에 붙은 M&M 초콜릿들이 스스로 재배열되어 새로운 모양이 되었습니다. 그것은 이렇게 쓰여 있었습니다:

증말 바보가튼 질무니네(A REALLY DUMB QUESTION)

"믿을 수가 없어요." 저는 아빠에게 속삭였습니다. "우리는 죽은 사람하고 실제로 대화하고 있어요!"

"죽은 사람일 뿐만 아니라." 아빠가 말했습니다. "맞춤법에 맞게 글을 쓰지 못하는 죽은 사람과 대화하는 거지." 적어도 아빠는 자신의 예전 모습이 되어 말하는 것 같았습니다.

"오, 유령이여." 제가 말했습니다. "당신은 왜 이런 일들을 우리에게 하고 있나요?"

조용하고, 긁는 것 같은 소리가 우리 머리 위에서 더 났고, 그다음에 M&M 초콜릿이 새롭게 배열되었습니다:

솔직히 나는 심심해 그리고 이거슨 재미있어(FRANKLY I'M BORED AND IT'S FUN)

"그렇지만 당신은 우리 집의 모든 가구와 접시와 물건들을 망가뜨리고 있어요." 저는 말했습니다. "당신이 계속 이렇게 하면, 우리 집엔 남아나는 게 없을 것입니다."

어쩌겠어 그거시 내 일이야(TOUGH IT'S MY JOB)

"당신 일이라고요?" 제가 말했습니다. "당신의 일이 무엇입니까?"

조용하고, 긁히는 소리가 더 났습니다.

장남치고, 잠난도 하고, 잔난하고

84 A GHOST NAMED WANDA

오 젠장 집어치워 엉망진창으로 만두는 거야(TO BE MISHEVUSS MISCHIVISS MISCHEFUSS O THE HECK WITH IT TO MAKE A MESS OF THINGS)

이 악령이 죽은 사람이든 산 사람이든, 제가 지금까지 만났던 사람들 중에서 가장 맞춤법이 엉망이었습니다.

"아빠, 무엇을 더 물어보아야 할지 모르겠어요." 저는 속삭였습니다.

"우리가 누구와 이야기하고 있는 것인지 알아내야 해." 아빠가 말했습니다.

"오, 유령이시여, 당신의 이름은 무엇입니까?" 제가 물었습니다. "제 말은, 무슨 이름으로 당신을 부르나요?"

M&M 초콜릿이 한 번 더 빠르게 배열되었습니다:

완다(WANDA)

"완다?" 저는 따라서 말했습니다. "그렇지만 완다는 여자 이름인데요."

그래서 뭐(SO WHAT)

"당신은 여자입니까?" 제가 물었습니다.

그렇다 왜(SO WHAT)

"어, 부인, 당신은 몇 백 살쯤 되었나요?" 제가 물었습니다.

8 정도(ABOUT 8)

"당신은 팔백 세입니까?" 저는 정중하게 말했습니다.

아니 그냥 8살이라고 바부야 8살하고 도 반이야 곧 9살이 되지(NO JUST 8 SILLY 8 AND A HALF GOING ON 9)

"여덟 살 반?" 제가 말했습니다. "아빠, 아이였어요! 애가 우리 아파트를 엉망으로 만들고 있었어요!"

"음, 말이 되는 것 같구나." 아빠가 말했습니다. "내 말은, 땅콩 M&M 초콜릿을 이용해서 말하고 맞춤법도 모르는 죽은 사람들과 대화하는 정도로 말이 된다는 뜻이야."

"네가 죽었다면." 저는 말했습니다. "너는 왜 천국이나 그런 비슷한 곳에 있지 않니?"

들어가는 대기 명단이 길어(LONG WAITING LIST TO GET IN)

"너는 어쩌다가 이 집을 엉망으로 만들기로 했니?" 제가 물었습니다.

나 전에 어기 살앗어(I USED TO LIVE HERE)

"네가 이 건물에 살았었다고?" 아빠가 말했습니다.

그래 삼심 년 전 쯤에 나는 여기를 싫어했어(YEAH ABOUT THIRTY YEARS AGO I HATED IT)

"왜 싫어했는데?" 제가 물었습니다.

그때 놀 사람이 업었어 게다가 칭구도 하나도 업었지(NOBODY TO PLAY WITH THEN EITHER NOBODY WAS MY FRIEND)

번역

제가 완다에게 다음에는 뭐라고 말할지 생각해 내려고 애쓰고 있었는데, 그때 갑자기 저의 게임 보이(Game Boy)가 공중을 가로지르며 날아갔습니다. 그것은 벽에 부딪혀서 산산조각이 났습니다. 저는 제 게임 보이를 정말 좋아했습니다. 저는 거기에 들어 있는 "틴 마스터즈 오브 더 갤럭시(Teen Masters of the Galaxy)" 게임에서 거의 29단계까지 갔었습니다. 이제 그건 완전히 다 사라져 버렸습니다.

"완다, 이 바보야, 너 왜 그랬어?" 저는 소리쳤습니다.

천장의 M&M 초콜릿이 다시 저절로 움직여 재배열되었습니다:

그냥 그러고 싶었어 심심해졌거든 (JUST FELT LIKE IT GOT BORED)

"너 내가 무슨 생각하는지 알아?" 제가 말했습니다. "너는 말썽쟁이고 멍청이야. 너는 심지어 네가 죽기 전에도 문제아에 멍청이였을거야. 그래서 너에게 친구가 없었던 거야. 네가 계속 멍청이 짓을 하고 있어서 죽은 뒤 남은 삶에서도 앞으로도 친구가 절대로 없을 거라고!"

6장

"완다는 불행한 아이 같구나." 아빠는 말했습니다. "아마도 내가 그녀와 이야기를 해 보아야겠어."

"그러세요." 제가 말했습니다. 저는 앉아서 팔짱을 꼈습니다. 저는 완다와 더 이상 아무것도 하고 싶지 않았습니다.

"완다야." 아빠가 아주 차분한 목소리로, 말했습니다. "내 생각에 너는 틀림없이 화가 나서 우리 아파트를 엉망으로 만든 것 같구나."

하하하 아저씨 생각을 누가 궁금해 하겠어 (HA HA HA WHO EVEN CARES WHAT YOU THINK)

"너는 무슨 일 때문에 그렇게 화가 났니?" 아빠는 계속 말했습니다.

나는 주것서 (I'M DEAD)

"자 그럼, 가서 다른 착한 죽은 여자애들과 놀고 우리 집은 좀 내버려 둬!" 저는 소리를 지르지 않을 수 없었습니다.

주변에 아무도 업서 (THERE AIN'T NO ONE AROUND)

"설마!" 제가 말했습니다.

"잭, 너는 전혀 도움이 안 되고 있어." 아빠가 날카로운 목소리로 지적했습니다. 그런 뒤 아빠는 천장으로 다시 고개를 돌렸습니다. "완다야, 우리가 무엇을 하면 되겠니?" 아빠는 물었습니다.

잠시 아무 대답이 없었습니다. 그런

뒤 M&M 초콜릿들이 한 번 더 저절로 재배열됐습니다:

나는 잭이 나랑 놀아 줬으면 좋겠어 (I WANT ZACK TO PLAY WITH ME)

저는 깜짝 놀랐습니다. 저는 그 말을 믿을 수 없었습니다.

"도대체 내가 왜 내 장난감을 망가뜨리고 우리 아빠의 아파트를 엉망으로 만드는 사람이랑 놀고 싶겠어?" 저는 말했습니다. "너는 내가 미쳤다고 생각하니? 나는 나한테 잘해 주고 내 물건을 잘 다루는 사람들하고만 놀아. 그리고 넌 분명 그런 사람이 아니야!"

다시 한 번 완다는 느리게 대답했습니다. M&M 초콜릿들이 움직여서 새로운 글자들의 조합으로 바뀌었습니다:

내가 고칠 쑤 있으면 어떡할래(WHAT IF I COULD FIX IT)

저는 아빠를 바라보았습니다. 아빠는 엉망이 된 우리 아파트를 둘러보았고 슬프게 고개를 저었습니다.

"완다야." 제가 말했습니다. "이곳은 전쟁터 같아. 네가 우리 아파트에 한 일들은 고칠 수 있는 수준을 넘어섰어."

내기 할래(WANNA BET)

"좋아." 제가 말했습니다.

얼마(HOW MUCH)

"25센트." 제가 말했습니다. 저는 25센트 동전을 꺼내서 그것을 들어 올렸습니다. "여기 내 돈 있어."

제가 들고 있던 25센트 동전이 따끔거리더니 분해되었습니다. 그러더니 눈을 뜰 수 없을 정도의 빛이 나왔습니다. 제 게임 보이의 모든 조각들이 다시 날아와서 합쳐졌습니다. 그것은 마치 TV 광고에서 영상을 거꾸로 돌렸을 때 누군가가 수영장 밖으로 나와서, 다이빙대 위로 되돌아가는 장면 같았습니다.

"세상에." 제가 말했습니다. "너 그거 어떻게 한 거야?"

비법이 잇지(TRICK OF THE TRADE)

"내 말 들어 봐, 완다, 넌 네가 망가뜨린 나머지 물건들도 고칠 수 있겠니?" 아빠가 희망에 찬 목소리로 말했습니다.

조건이 있어(THAT DEPENDS)

"무슨 조건?"

잭이 나에게 무엇을 해 주는지에 달렸어(ON WHAT ZACK DOES FOR ME)

저는 아빠를 바라보았습니다. 아빠는 어깨를 으쓱했습니다. 그때 저에게 좋은 생각이 났습니다. 저는 완다와 놀고 싶지 않다고 생각했습니다. 완다는 분명 제가 좋아하는 유형이 아닙니다. 죽은 것도 그렇고 말이에요. 그렇지만...

"애, 완다." 제가 말했습니다. "네가 망가뜨린 나머지 물건들도 고쳐 주면,

번역

너에게 적절한 놀이 친구를 내가 찾아 줄 수 있을 거야."

너를 말하는 거겠지(YOU MEAN YOU)

"아니 아니, 나 말고. 나보다 더 나은 사람. 영혼 세계에 있는 누군가 말이야. 어떻게 생각해?"

대답이 없었습니다. 저는 완다가 제 말을 들었는지 궁금했습니다. 그때 마치 큰 지진이 시작되려는 것처럼, 방이 흔들리기 시작했습니다. 모래 폭풍 속에 있는 것처럼, 아파트 전체가 조금 희뿌옇게 되었습니다. 그러고 나서 갑자기 물건들이 공중에 날아다니기 시작했습니다. 접시, 은식기. 그릇. 냄비. 옷. 책. 텔레비전 세트까지. 시끄러운 소리가 났습니다. 긁히는 소리. 갈리는 소리. 쨍그랑거리는 소리.

무거운 책이 제 왼쪽 어깨에 부딪쳐서 튕겨나갔습니다. 엑토플라즘 방울이 제 뺨에 떨어졌습니다. 작은 접시가 마치 비행접시처럼 제 귀를 스쳐 날아갔습니다. 생각해보니, 그건 정말 날아다니는 접시였습니다.

그러고 나서, 그 일들이 시작되었던 것처럼 갑자기, 끝났습니다. 안개가 걷혔습니다. 아빠와 저는 아파트를 둘러보았습니다. 우리는 우리의 눈을 믿을 수 없었습니다.

끈적거리는 엑토플라즘은 완전히 사라졌습니다. 주방도 모두 깨끗이 치워져 있었습니다. 제 방은, 깔끔하다고 할 수 없는 상태였습니다. 하지만 확실히 완다가 손대기 전보다 더 엉망은 아니었습니다.

저는 너무 기뻐서 소리를 지르고 싶었습니다. 제 아빠는 마치 방금 복권에 당첨이라도 된 것처럼 보였습니다.

"완다야, 네가 해냈어!" 제가 말했습니다. "네가 정말 해냈어!"

내가 뭐랬어(I TOLD YOU)

"좋아." 제가 말했습니다. "넌 네가 한 말을 지켰어. 그러니 이번엔 내가 한 말을 내가 지킬 차례야. 나를 따라와."

우리 어디 가는데(WHERE ARE WE GOING)

"가 보면 알아." 제가 말했습니다.

7장

아빠는 아파트가 다시 원래 상태로 돌아온 것에 너무 기뻐서, 제가 버논의 집에 가게 두었습니다. 그리고 제가 버논에게 전화를 걸어서 그의 폴터가이스트 문제를 도와주러 제가 갈 거라고 했을 때, 그는 그 말을 믿으려 하지 않았습니다.

그래서 저는 흑마술에 대한 저의 책과 제 검은 양초 일곱 개를 가져갔습니다다. 그리고 저는 길을 건널 때 양쪽을 살피면서, 버논의 집을 향해 세 블록을 걸어갔습니다. 저는 완다에게 계속 말을 걸었습니다. 저는 그녀가 저를 따라오고 있는지 확인하고 싶었습니다. 당연히, 저는 그녀를 볼 수 없었습니다. 그리고 주변에 M&M 초콜릿도 없었기 때문에, 그녀는 저에게 "말을 걸" 수 없었습니다. 거리에서 제가 지나친 사람들은 제가 그곳에 없는 누군가에게 이야기하는 것을 보았습니다. 그들은 마치 제가 정신 나간 사람인 것처럼 저를 쳐다보았습니다.

"야, 완다." 제가 말했습니다. "네가 아직 내 옆에 있으면, 나에게 신호를 줘."

챙이 넓은 밀짚모자를 쓴, 아주 고지식해 보이는 어떤 부인이, 저를 향해 걸어오고 있었습니다. 갑자기 무언가 그녀의 밀짚모자 챙을 붙잡아서 그녀의 눈을 덮도록 그것을 잡아당겼습니다. 그래요! 완다가 아직 저와 함께 있네요!

두껍고, 냄새 나는 시가(cigar)를 피우는 한 남자가 이 장면을 보고 웃기 시작했습니다. 그리고 그때 그의 시가가 불꽃을 일으키며 폭발하더니, 그의 얼굴이 검댕으로 뒤덮였습니다.

얼마 지나지 않아 저는 버논의 아파트에 도착했습니다. 버논의 부모님은 부자였습니다. 5번가에 있는 그들의 큰 아파트는 커다란 소파, 유리로 된 거대한 탁자, 그리고 거대하고 불편한 의자들로 채워져 있었습니다. 그들의 가구 대부분에는 투명한 플라스틱 커버가 덮여 있었습니다. 아마도 버논의 부모님도 그만큼 땀을 많이 흘리나 봅니다.

즉시 저는 문제점을 알아차렸습니다. 그의 아파트는 아파트들이 그래야 하는 것보다 훨씬 더 깔끔했습니다. 탁자 위의 모든 잡지들은 처음에는 크기순으로, 다음에는 날짜순으로, 계속해서 저절로 재배열되고 있었습니다. 그리고 아무도 그것을 들고 있는 사람이 없는 걸레가 현관에 있는 모든 고급 물건들의 광을 내고 있었습니다.

"야, 버논." 제가 불렀습니다. "너 어디 있어?"

제가 그 말을 하자마자, 걸레는 광을 내는 것을 멈췄고 복도를 따라 둥둥 떠갔습니다. 그것은 아파트 뒤쪽으로 가고 있었습니다. 저는 따라가야 한다는 것을 깨달았습니다.

버논은 부엌에서 알파벳 수프를 후루룩 마시면서, 저녁을 먹고 있었습니다. 제가 보는 사이, 수프 안의 글자들이 계속 저절로 재배열되어서 그것들은 완벽한 알파벳 순서로 그의 숟가락 안으로 들어가고 있었습니다.

"잭, 저녁 좀 먹겠니?" 그의 엄마가 물었습니다.

번역

"아뇨 괜찮아요, 만토이펠 아주머니. 제 생각에 우리는 바로 일을 해야 할 것 같아요."

우리는 검은색 양초 일곱 개에 불을 붙였습니다. 그런 뒤 저는 흑마술에 대한 책을 펴서 퇴치 의식을 다시 읽기 시작했습니다: "오, 사악한 유령이여, 오, 더러운 곳에 거주하며, 어둡고, 냄새나는 곳에 살고 있는 위대하고 끔찍한 악령이여. . ."

갑자기 작은 폭발이 일어났습니다. 종이 한 장이 부엌 식탁 위로 떨어졌고, 펜 한 자루가 책상 서랍에서 나와서 날아왔고 아주 화려한 필기체로 뭔가 쓰기 시작했습니다.

"제발 나를 모욕하지 마세요." 그것은 썼습니다. "나는 사악하지 않아요. 나는 더러운 곳에 살지 않아요. 그리고 나는 확실히 어둡고, 냄새나는 곳에 살지도 않는다고요!"

버논과 그의 엄마는 펜이 종이 위에 글씨를 쓰는 것을 지켜보았습니다. 그들의 눈이 그들의 머리에서 거의 튀어나올 것처럼 커졌습니다.

"버논." 그의 엄마가 말했습니다. "네가 마술을 할 줄 아는 줄 몰랐구나. 너 그거 어떻게 한 거니?"

"그건 제가 한 것이 아니에요!" 버논이 말했습니다.

"용서해 주세요, 유령님." 제가 말했습니다. "당신이 정말 깨끗하고 깔끔하다는 걸 알 수 있어요. 당신의 이름은 무엇인가요?"

"나를 세실(Cecil)이라고 불러도 좋아요." 펜이 썼습니다. "그리고 당신을 뭐라고 불러야 할까요, 선생님?"

"저는 잭이에요." 제가 말했습니다. 지금까지 저를 "선생님"이라고 부른 사람은 없었습니다. 저는 그게 조금 마음에 들었습니다.

"당신을 알게 되어 기뻐요, 잭." 펜이 썼습니다. "그런데 당신은 누구를 데려왔죠? 저는 다른 유령이 있다는 것을 느낄 수 있어요."

작은 폭발이 한 번 더 일어났습니다. 치리오스(Cheerios) 시리얼 상자가 부엌 찬장 밖으로 떨어졌습니다. 내용물들은 버논이 저녁을 먹고 있는 식탁 위로 날아갔습니다. 버논, 그의 엄마, 그리고 제가 보고 있을 때, 치리오스는 스스로 배열되어 말을 이루었습니다:

얘 세실 나는 완다야 안농(HEY CECIL I'M WADNA HOW ARE YOU DOING)

8장

펜은 완다에게 메시지를 휘갈겨 쓰기 시작했습니다. 그리고 치리오스는 계속 저절로 재배열되어서 세실에게 메시지를 쓰고 있었습니다. 휘갈겨 쓰는 것과 재배열되는 것은 점점 빨라졌습니다. 곧 그것들은 살아 있는 사람들이 따라가기에 너무 빨라졌습니다.

"음." 제가 말했습니다. "제가 보기에 이 둘은 서로 마음이 통한 것 같은데요."

끄적거림과 치리오스의 재배열은 갑자기 멈추었습니다. 그러더니 치리오스는 제가 읽을 수 있을 만큼 천천히 다음과 같은 말을 만들어 냈습니다:

그건 네 생각이고(THAT'S WHAT YOU THINK)

"네 말은 너희가 서로를 좋아하지 않는다는 거야?" 제가 말했습니다.

펜이 다시 갈겨쓰기 시작했습니다.

"당신 친구 완다는 버릇없고, 교양 없으며, 그리고 받아들이기 힘들 만큼 지저분한 사람입니다." 펜은 썼습니다.

치리오스가 움직이기 시작했습니다.

네 친구 세실은 잘난 체하는 사람이야(YOUR FRIEND CECIL IS A SNOB)

"얘들아, 자, 진정해." 제가 말했습니다. "너희 둘은 공통점이 많아, 죽었다는 것을 포함해서 말이야."

"맞아, 너네 둘은 친구가 *되어야 해!*" 버논이 덧붙였습니다.

버넌 너는 땀 많이 흘리는 멍충이야(VERNON YOU ARE A JERK WHO SWEATS A LOT) 라고 치리오스가 말했습니다.

"야!" 의자에서 일어나며, 버논이 말했습니다. "그 말 취소해!"

갑자기 버논의 바지가 신발까지 확 잡아당겨져 내려갔습니다. 그는 보라색 공룡이 그려진 팬티를 입고 있었습니다. 그는 바지를 다시 위로 끌어올리려고 얼른 몸을 숙였습니다. 그러나 버논의 손이 닿기도 전에, 그것은 난폭하게 다리 위로 올려져서 다시 제자리로 돌아갔습니다. 그리고 그의 셔츠는 보이지 않는 손에 의해 바지 속으로 단단히 들어갔습니다.

"그만해!" 버논이 말했습니다.

"멈춰!" 버논의 엄마가 말했습니다.

버논의 바지는 한 번 더 그의 신발까지 아래로 잡아당겨졌습니다. 그리고 다시 위로 올라갔습니다. 그리고 그만큼이나 빠르게 아래로 다시 내려갔습니다.

"완다! 세실! 당장 그만둬!" 제가 외쳤습니다.

그 소리는 아빠가 정말 화가 났을 때 소리 지르는 것보다 훨씬 더 컸습니다. 그것은 버논과 제가 교실에서 싸울 때 호프만 선생님이 소리치는 것보다 더 컸습니다. 그것은 너무 커서 버논과 그의 엄마는 충격으로 입을 다물었습니다.

번역

저는 완다와 세실도 놀랐다고 생각했는데, 왜냐하면 버논의 바지가 요요처럼 그의 다리에서 위아래로 왔다갔다 하며 움직이던 것이 멈췄기 때문입니다. 버논은 바지를 다시 끌어올렸고 자리에 앉았습니다.

"훨씬 낫네." 제가 말했습니다. "너희 둘은 죽었을지 몰라도, 아기처럼 행동하고 있어. 그리고 나는 그것을 용납하지 않을 거야."

호프만 선생님은 "용납하다"라는 말을 쓰는 것을 정말 좋아합니다. 왜 그런지 저도 알겠어요.

"좋아." 저는 말했습니다. "있지, 너희 둘은 좋은 친구가 될 수 있을 거야. 그런데 너희는 어울리는 법을 배워야 해. 하려고 하면, 할 수 있어. 내 말은 버논과 나도 지금은 잘 지내고 있잖아. 게다가 우리는 서로를 좋아하지도 않아."

"야!" 버논이 말했습니다. 그는 상처받은 것 같았습니다.

"내 말은 전에는 친하지 않았다는 거였어." 제가 말했습니다. "어쨌든, 너희는 잘 지내야 해. 너희에게 선택의 여지가 없어. 동네에는 죽은 애들이 그렇게 많지 않거든. 또한, 너희는 지낼 곳을 찾아야 해."

우리가 너네 집으로 이사하면 되잖아 잭(HOW ABOUT WE MOVE IN WITH YOU ZACK)

"그래, 잭." 버논이 말했습니다. "그거 좋은 생각이다."

"미안한데, 얘들아." 제가 말했습니다. "절대 안 돼."

"우리 둘이 버논하고 같이 사는 건 어때?" 펜이 끄적거렸습니다.

"오, 그거 재미있는 생각이다." 제가 말했습니다.

"안 돼!" 자리에서 펄쩍 뛰며, 버논이 외쳤습니다. 잠깐이었지만, 저는 버논이 자기 바지를 다시 잃어 버릴 것 같다고 생각했습니다.

"좋아, 얘들아, 나에게 좋은 생각이 있어." 제가 말했습니다. "너희 강 바로 건너 뉴저지(New Jersey)에 있는 어드벤처랜드(Adventureland) 놀이공원을 아니? 음, 거기 정말 한심한 유령의 집이 있어. 그곳은 다섯 살짜리조차 겁주지 못하거든. 하지만 너희 같은 전문가 두 명이라면 당장에 그곳을 제대로 돌려놓을 수 있을 거야. 아니, 너희 둘이 거기서 나타나기 시작하면, 그곳은 누구에게든 잔뜩 겁을 줄 수 있을 거라고 장담해."

아니면 바지가 벗겨질 만큼 겁을 주거나(OR THE PANTS)

"그래." 제가 말했습니다. "어떻게 생각해, 얘들아? 어드벤처랜드로 이사할래?"

처음에는 답이 없었습니다. 그리고

그때: "내 생각에 어드벤처랜드에서 유령의 집을 차지하는 것은 정말 재미있는 도전이 될 것 같아." 펜이 썼습니다.

버논과 그의 엄마는 안도하는 것처럼 보였습니다.

"완다, 네 생각은 어때?" 제가 말했습니다.

너네 우리 보러 와 주거야(WOULD YOU COME TO VISIT US)

"어, 그래, 당연하지." 제가 말했습니다. "물론 우리가 갈게, 완다. 우리에게 기회가 있을 때마다 우리는 너희를 보러 갈게."

너네 우리 보러 안 오믄 우리가 너네 보러 가꺼야(IF YOU DON'T VISIT US THEN I GUESS WE'LL HAVE TO VISIT YOU)

"우리가 보러 갈 거야, 우리가 간다고." 제가 말했습니다.

그렇게 완다와 세실은 어드벤처랜드에 있는 유령의 집에서 살기 위해 떠났습니다. 저는 그들이 어울려서 지낼 방법을 찾았는지 궁금합니다! 가끔씩 뉴스를 통해, 저는 그곳에서 이상한 일이 일어난다는 소식을 듣습니다. 모든 사람들은 어드벤처랜드를 운영하는 사람들이 새로운 으스스한 장난을 개발해 냈다고 생각합니다. 그렇지만 저는 정말로 누가 그 배후에 있는지 알고 있지요.

그리고 저는 완다에게 한 약속을 지킬 것입니다. 우리는 어드벤처랜드에 있는 유령의 집에서 큰 파티를 열어서 제 돌아오는 생일을 축하할 것입니다.

분명 재미있는 파티가 될 것입니다. 실제로, 정말 재미있을 것입니다.

ANSWER KEY

Chapter 1

1. A One night a few months ago, I woke up suddenly. All the doors in our apartment kept on opening and closing. The door to Dad's room, my bedroom door, my bathroom door, the door to my closet. Just opening and closing by themselves. I figured, hey, no big deal. It's the wind or something.

2. B My room is always pretty messy. But this morning, it was a lot messier than usual. The pants I had taken off the night before and thrown on the floor were now hanging from the roller of the window shade. The shoes I had tossed in the corner were in my wastebasket. My T-shirt was hanging from the light on the ceiling. My underpants were on my teddy bear's head.

3. D I cleaned up the stuff as fast as I could. It wasn't so much because I like my room clean. I just didn't want my dad to come in and say, "What's wrong with this picture?"

4. C I went back into my bedroom, and my mouth dropped open. My room was a mess again.

5. D The look on my dad's face told me he still wasn't buying it. But at that precise moment, the TV that sits on top of my bookcase floated gently into the air. Then it flew slowly and silently across the room and landed on my dresser. My dad watched it go. His eyes were very wide. So were mine. "You know, Zack," said my dad after a long time, "I think I believe you after all."

Chapter 2

1. B Dad and I ran out of my room and escaped into the kitchen. We blocked the door with a stepladder.

2. C The table was already set for breakfast. The only thing was, it was set upside down. All the dishes were piled up in one very tall stack, which was swaying unsteadily back and forth.

3. A There was no longer any doubt about it. We had a poltergeist. I've read books about this stuff, and I know. But in case you don't, a poltergeist is like a ghost. A ghost that likes to cause trouble. They usually appear in homes with families that have at least one kid, and they trash the place.

4. C "What would you think of our staying in the Ramada Inn tonight?" asked my dad.

5. D The very tall stack of dishes teetered in one direction, then in the other. Then it collapsed with a very loud crash. Pieces of smashed dishes flew in all directions. The refrigerator door sprang open, and all the food inside spilled out onto the floor. "On the other hand," I said, "I hear those Ramada Inns can be really nice."

Chapter 3

1. D I kept thinking about ghosts. Who even knew what was going on now in my dad's apartment? I was thinking so hard about ghosts that I must have totally tuned out what we were doing in class.

2. D "What's on your mind today that's more important than schoolwork?"

3. B The kids in class were laughing so hard they almost fell out of their chairs. "Oh, right, Zack," said some, and, "Yeah, sure, Zack."

4. C Vernon Manteuffel sweats a lot and only takes baths on weekends. He keeps his bubble gum behind his ear. He brags that his gym clothes haven't been washed since the third grade. He's kind of a school legend.

5. A "You know, although I don't believe in the supernatural, there are a great many people who do. And they are not all superstitious barfbags either, Vernon. What I suggest, Zack, is that you go to the library and do a little research."

Chapter 4

1. C "We have ghosts the way some people have cockroaches." "Then what you want is a banishing ritual," he said. "Banishing rituals are the Roach Motels of the spirit world. You'll find them under black magic over there under the stairway."

2. D I read all about poltergeists. In one book on black magic, I finally found a

ANSWER KEY

banishing ritual. You were supposed to light seven black candles and say this seven times: "O evil spirit, O great and terrible demon that dwelleth in filth, that liveth in dark, stinking places, hear me now: I cast you out! I command you to depart! I order that you leaveth this place!"

3. A "Then why are you checking out books on ghosts?" "If I tell you, do you promise to keep it a secret?" "Maybe." "Here's the thing," Vernon said, looking around nervously and lowering his voice to a whisper. "Something weird is going on in my apartment, too."

4. D "You don't understand," he said. "Things in my room are being invisibly rearranged. Not the way I want them, but the way something else wants them."

5. B I left Vernon on the steps of the library. If the banishing ritual worked for me, maybe I'd show Vernon how to do it too.

Chapter 5

1. B Things in the apartment had gotten a lot worse. Not only was the place completely trashed, but there was clear gooey stuff all over everything.

2. C "O spirit who dwelleth in this place," I said in a low, respectful tone. "Are you the same spirit who hath trashed our apartment?" There were soft, scraping sounds as the M&Ms on the ceiling rearranged themselves into a new pattern. It said: A RILLY DUM QUESCHUN

3. A "O spirit," I said, "why dost thou doeth these things to us?" There were more soft, scratching sounds above our heads, and then a new arrangement of M&Ms: FRANKLY IM BORD ALSO ITS FUN

4. D "You lived in this building?" said my dad. YEH ABOUT THIRDY YEARS AGO I HATED IT "Why did you hate it?" I asked. NOBODY TO PLAY WITH THEN ETHER NOBODY WAS MY FREND

5. B "You know what I think?" I said. "I think you're a troublemaker and a jerk. I think you were a troublemaker and a jerk even before you were dead."

Chapter 6

1. C "What do you think could be making you so angry?" my dad went on. IM DED "Well then, why don't you go and play with some nice dead girls and leave us alone!" I couldn't help yelling. THERE AINT NONE AROUND "Tough!" I said. "Zack, you're not being helpful," Dad pointed out in a sharp voice. Then he turned his face back to the ceiling. "Wanda, what can we do?" he asked.

2. C "Why the heck would I ever want to play with somebody who destroys my toys and wrecks my dad's apartment?" I said. "You think I'm nuts? I only play with people who treat me nicely and who treat my stuff nicely. And that sure isn't you!"

3. D I looked at my dad. He looked around our wrecked apartment and shook his head sadly. "Wanda," I said, "this place looks like a war zone. What you've done to our apartment is beyond fixing."

4. B "Hey, Wanda," I said, "if you fix the rest of the stuff you broke, I might just be able to find you a possible playmate." YOU MEAN YOU "No no, not me. Better than me. Somebody in the spirit world. What do you say?"

5. A My dad and I looked around the apartment. We couldn't believe our eyes. The gooey ectoplasm was completely gone. The kitchen was all cleaned up, too. In my room, things weren't what you would call neat. But it was certainly no messier than before Wanda had gone to work.

Chapter 7

1. D I kept talking to Wanda. I wanted to make sure she was following me. I couldn't see her, of course. And because there were no M&Ms around, she couldn't "talk" to me. People I passed on the street saw me speaking to somebody who wasn't there. They looked at me like I was cuckoo.

2. C "Yo, Wanda," I said, "if you're still with me, give me a sign." A very stuffy-looking lady, wearing a straw hat with a wide brim, was walking toward me. All of a sudden something grabbed the brim of her straw hat and yanked it

ANSWER KEY

down over her eyes. Yep! Wanda was still with me!

3. A All the magazines on the coffee table kept rearranging themselves, first by size and then by date. And a dust rag with nobody holding it was polishing all the fancy stuff in the front hall.

4. D A piece of paper dropped onto the kitchen table, and a pen flew out of a desk drawer and began writing in a very fancy handwriting. "Kindly do not insult me," it wrote. "I am not evil. I do not dwell in filth. And I most certainly do not live in dark, stinking places!"

5. B A box of Cheerios fell out of a kitchen cupboard. Its contents flew onto the table where Vernon was eating his dinner. As Vernon, his mother, and I watched, the Cheerios arranged themselves into words: HEY CECIL IM WANDA HOWYA DOIN

Chapter 8

1. A The pen began to scribble again. "Your friend Wanda is a crude, uneducated, and unacceptably messy person," it wrote. The Cheerios came alive. YOUR FREND CECIL IS A SNOB

2. B "Wanda! Cecil! Stop it this instant!" I shouted. It was louder than my dad yells when he's really angry. It was louder than Mr. Hoffman yelled when Vernon and I had our fight in class. It was so loud that Vernon and his mother were shocked into silence. I guess Wanda and Cecil were too, because Vernon's pants stopped moving up and down his legs like a yo-yo. He pulled them back up again and sat down. "That's better," I said. "You two may be dead, but you're acting like babies. And I will not tolerate it."

3. C "Anyway, you have to get along. You don't have any choice. There just aren't that many dead kids in the neighborhood."

4. A "You know the Adventureland Amusement Park right across the river in New Jersey? Well, they've got a haunted house in it that is really pathetic. It couldn't even scare a five-year-old. But a couple of pros like you could really whip it into shape in no time. Why, after you two start haunting it, I'll bet that place could scare the daylights out of anybody."

5. D And so Wanda and Cecil went off to live in the haunted house at Adventureland. I wonder if they found a way to get along! Every once in a while on the news, I hear about strange things going on out there. Everybody thinks the people who run Adventureland just dreamed up some new spooky tricks. But I know who's really behind it.

Workbook text copyright © 2020 Longtail Books
Text copyright © 1996 by Dan Greenburg. All rights reserved.
First published in the United States by Grosset & Dunlap, Inc., a member of Penguin Putnam Books for Young Readers under the title A GHOST NAMED WANDA.
Korean and English rights arranged with Sheldon Fogelman Agency, Inc. through KCC(Korea Copyright Center Inc.), Seoul.

완다라는 이름의 유령
(A Ghost Named Wanda)

1판 1쇄 2020년 3월 13일
2판 1쇄 2025년 3월 3일

지은이   Dan Greenburg
기획   이수영
책임편집 정소이
편집   박새미 배주윤
콘텐츠제작및감수 롱테일 교육 연구소
저작권   명채린
마케팅   두잉글 사업 본부

펴낸이   이수영
펴낸곳   롱테일북스
출판등록 제2015-000191호
주소   04033 서울특별시 마포구 양화로 113, 3층(서교동, 순흥빌딩)
전자메일 help@ltinc.net

ISBN 979-11-93992-36-4 14740